LAST MAN STANDING.

Jesus and the fight for a generation

Michael John Meyers

© 2013 by Michael J. Meyers.
ISBN-13: 978-1499387537
ISBN-10: 1499387539

All rights reserved. No part of this publication may be reproduced, stored in a retrieval system, or transmitted in any form or by any means - for example, electronic, photo-copy, recording - without the prior written permission of the author. The only exception is brief quotations in printed reviews.

All scripture quotations, unless otherwise noted, are taken from THE HOLY BIBLE, NEW INTERNATIONAL VERSION®, NIV® Copyright © 1973, 1978, 1984, 2011 by Biblica, Inc.® Used by permission. All rights reserved worldwide.

If I could relive my life, I would devote my entire ministry to reaching children for God!

- Dwight L. Moody

Thank you for your heart for the children of Brazil!

Table of Contents

Acknowledgements *9*

Introduction - "Knock-Down, Drag-Out" *11*

Chapter 1 - Turning One Heart to the Children *19*

Chapter 2 - What GOD knows, Satan exploits, and the church has forgotten *49*

Chapter 3 - Defenses Down *81*

Chapter 4 - God is in your corner so come out swinging! ... *111*

Chapter 5 - Of Bull Elephants and Shark Wranglers *123*

Chapter 6 - "A defender of widows" *143*

Chapter 7 - "He places the lonely in families" *155*

Chapter 8 - Open Hearts, Open Arms *173*

Discussion Questions *191*

About Open Arms Worldwide *195*

About the Author *197*

Prologue

In December of 2000 I was resurrected from the dead. Not all of me at once mind you. As every believer in Jesus experiences, the "new creation" is a work in progress as God's resurrection power reanimates His image and likeness in each of us. At that time I was a compassion flat line. That all changed in an instant through a chance encounter with a homeless child, whose name I will never know, on a street in the heart of São Paulo, Brazil. In one amazing moment of answered prayer my heart of stone was replaced with a heart of flesh. That is where my story began.

I came of age in the 1990's, an era where so much had been written about what makes a godly man. He is courageous. He's a leader, a teacher, a provider and friend. He's a man of integrity. He is a faithful husband and loving father. I was deeply influenced by great Pastors and authors like Stu Webber, Dr. James Dobson and Josh McDowell. They woke me up to the high calling of fatherhood. I read them with a deep spiritual hunger, and I hope became a better father and husband, but their wisdom led me further, to a place I had never expected to go.

Exposure to the disintegration of civil society at home and around the world caused me to question if it is enough to simply care for, physically and spiritually, our children and the children in our church family. Does God call us to more?

LAST MAN STANDING

Everything I began to learn about children in our families and the church led me inevitably to the answer. We must move beyond. *The fact is that the fatherless outside the church far outnumber our own children and seventy percent of the children born in the world today are born into non-Christian homes.*

The greatest battle that the men and families of the church face in the new century is the knockdown drag-out fight with Satan for the next generation.

This is the story of my journey, as well as the story of many other families and children whose lives have been impacted by a simple truth. We are to be imitators of God, as dearly loved children, and our God is a Father to the fatherless. He places the lonely in families. From the favelas of Brazil, to Washington DC, we share one conviction in common: the church of Christ is the "Last man standing" between the children and the plans of Satan.

Acknowledgements

No acknowledgement would be complete without first giving ultimate thanks to God through my Lord, Jesus Christ, through whom my life was made possible. The experiences, blessings, and adventures I have enjoyed are a direct result of His saving grace in my life.

Secondly I want to acknowledge my wife, Patricia. I was blessed, most undeservedly, with a brilliant and beautiful bride. Patricia has inspired me, urged me on, and kept me grounded. God has used her to make me a better man. Without her encouragement to write this book I'm afraid it would have remained on my "bucket" list. To my children, Michael, Raphael and Bela, you guys have been so great about sharing your Dad with so many children who needed one. It has been a blessing to see you grow up serving Christ by serving others. A special thanks to young Michael for his invaluable help in formatting this book as well! Your mind amazes me.

Then there is my big sister Lynn, whose editing gifts helped take this from a single stream of consciousness to the book it is today. As a reader you will owe her a big thank you as well. Thanks Sis!

To my mom, an amazing writer herself, for giving me her love of the written word, and to my dad for being there in the beginning to help build the foundation that would carry me through the rough spots.

LAST MAN STANDING

To Dolores Walker my Sunday school teacher who loved me like Jesus, and my neighbor, Phyllis Polhemus, who led me to close the deal with God at her backyard Bible club, thank you for your faithfulness to the Gospel and to your commitment to reaching children like me for Christ.

Then of course there are the many, many folks who have taken a chance on me, poured into my life and fought the good fight along with me. Some of them I have mentioned in the pages of this book, but certainly not all. Any attempt at naming them all here would without doubt end badly. You know who you are and I love and thank you.

Loved ones, your influence flows through the pages of this book and the pages of my life. Thank you!

Introduction - "Knock-Down, Drag-Out"

INTRODUCTION – KNOCK-DOWN, DRAG-OUT

Enough is enough

We are losing the next generation. Not just in our homes and not just in our churches or our country, but also around the world and in every segment of society. The deck is stacked against us. Pop culture, pornography, drugs, gangs, the secular assault on education, the social welfare state; and on and on. Add to this the fact that the godly man and father are vanishing from our culture. Fatherlessness has become an epidemic that is leaving no social class or culture untouched. We are losing ground fast. Our adversary is well funded, well-armed and has a head start. We, the Church, are the "last man standing" between the children of the world and the schemes of Satan. What can we do? What should we do? Can we afford to protect only our own and withdraw from the world, hiding within the walls of our church? Is this "circle the wagons" strategy really a godly solution?

What if we purposed in our hearts to do something different? There is a great scene in the 1981 film, "Coward of the County," based on a classic Kenny Rogers ballad, where Tommy, aptly nicknamed "Yellow" for his reputation for not standing up against the town bullies, finally has been pushed too far by three ruffians who have assaulted his girl. Tommy tracks the bad guys down at their favorite bar. Amid laughter upon Tommy's entrance, and after "one of them got up and met him halfway 'cross the floor", Tommy turns around, appearing to once again choose non-confrontation, when instead, "you coulda heard a pin drop when Tommy stopped and locked the door". Fueled by "twenty years of crawlin'" that "was bottled up inside him", Tommy engages in a relentless bar room brawl that leaves all three bad guys unconscious on the floor.

What if, instead of running from the fight for the children, we turned in the face of our enemies' laughter, locked the door and threw down on behalf of our own children and the children of the world? In Matthew 18:6, Jesus himself says, *"If anyone causes one of these little ones—those who believe in me—to stumble, it would be better for them to have a large millstone hung around their neck and to be drowned in the depths of the sea."* Them's fightin words if I've ever heard them.

The Minefield

Here is another way to look at it. The lights come up on the stage. It is strewn with armed bear traps, their solid steel jaws ready to snap shut, maiming and potentially killing their prey. On one side of the stage stands a child. The narrator begins dramatically,

"This maze of real bear traps on stage represents the obstacles and dangers that the world places in a child's path to adulthood. This young person will, in a moment be walking across this stage, through the traps, to represent the life journey she must undertake. But before she begins, we are missing one essential element to make our metaphor complete. In our youth we often lack

INTRODUCTION – KNOCK-DOWN, DRAG-OUT

wisdom and always lack full knowledge and understanding of the dangers that lie ahead. To represent this spiritual blindness, our child will be wearing a blindfold."

Now, with the blindfold firmly in place, the narrator begins the countdown for the child to begin her terrifying journey across a virtual mine field, blind; disaster seems unavoidable. "Three, two, one, Go!"

Suddenly another voice is heard, sharp and loud from offstage,

"Stop! Don't you move a muscle, I am coming to you."

The child freezes in place while a man appears from the opposite side of the stage and picks his way carefully through the traps until he stands at her side. He gently removes the blindfold, takes the child by the hand and leads her through the maze of traps, safely to the other side.

Thank you for investing just a bit of your life in the pursuit of wisdom regarding one of the most critical yet under-funded and misunderstood battles in the Kingdom of GOD, the battle for the hearts and souls of the next generation.

In these pages you will learn about the special place children hold in the heart of GOD and how, as His image bearers and imitators, we must hold them deeply in our hearts as well.

Through scripture, testimonies, and my personal story, we will prepare for the fight of our lives. We will discover the very unique way we as GOD's creation are "wired" and why that "wiring" makes it critical as parents and the church to reach children early with quality, relational discipleship. We will expose Satan's strategy for leaving the children in your family, church, neighborhood and around the world vulnerable to his plans and begin to understand why "real men," as well as women and families, must do children's ministry. Finally, we will look at what I believe is a Biblical call to action for the whole family of GOD.

It is my prayer that this book will serve as a starting point for leaders of the church, men of all ages and life stages, and their families to *reorder their priorities and take the lead in the fight for the next generation. The Church of Jesus Christ is the last man standing.*

A word to the ladies

Wives, sisters and mothers please don't close this book. Husbands, get your wife to read this section at least. With a title like "Last Man Standing" you might imagine that I will spend a lot of time in these pages addressing men and spurring them on to assume their GOD given roles as fathers, mentors, protectors and spiritual leaders. You would be correct, but that is only part of the story. This fight is truly a family affair.

INTRODUCTION – KNOCK-DOWN, DRAG-OUT

You hold the key

I praise GOD for the women of the Church. Thank you for doing your part in fending off Satan's attacks on the children. Were it not for you the situation could be far worse indeed, but you were never intended to shoulder this burden alone.

What the children of the world need today is not less of the female influence but rather an increase in the presence of godly men in their lives.

While I don't want to burden you further, I must share with you this truth; you hold an important key to mobilizing the godly man to join you in this fight. You can be a catalyst for moving the men in your life, whether that is your boyfriend, husband, brother, father or grandfather, beyond our culture's definition of manhood to a higher place. This is a family endeavor, so step out **with** them and be the kind of families GOD has designed you to be.

This may sound great to you at first glance, but it will require sacrifice. For you wives, you will need to release your husband and encourage him to not only be the spiritual leader in the home and of your children, but to take the next step and become a "Father to the fatherless" outside the home in your community and around the world.

What might that mean? You may need to sacrifice some of your time together to allow him to mentor a child from a broken home. It may mean another mouth to feed occasionally at the dinner table or having someone new participating in a family event. Perhaps it will mean that he starts "butting in" on your nighttime routine with the children. It could even be much more radical than any of these examples. Whatever form it takes, you must understand this truth; **you wield incredible power; power to either squash your husbands will to obey scripture or to fill his heart with courage to move out into uncharted territory.** *It is a rare man indeed who can live out his faith while his wife is resisting him at every turn.* The choice is yours.

I would like to challenge you to read these pages and prayerfully consider what Christ would have you do in response.

Are you ready?

Chapter 1 - Turning One Heart to the Children

CHAPTER 1 – TURNING ONE HEART TO THE CHILDREN

"And he shall turn the heart of the fathers to the children, and the heart of the children to their fathers, lest I come and smite the earth with a curse."

Malachi 4:6

In the coming chapters we will look at what I believe is a Biblical call to action for the family of GOD in relation to our own children, the children of our church, and at-risk children wherever we find them. That may seem like a heavy load, so before we go there, I'd like to share with you the story of how one man's heart was turned to the children and how it made him a better husband and more effective father. This story is nothing less than a testimony of the resurrection power of Jesus Christ. Let me explain.

The most unlikely missionary

In the class of 1989 at Point Pleasant Borough High in Point Pleasant NJ, had there been such a category, I might have been voted "Most <u>unlikely</u> to become a missionary." My parents were good people, a high school teacher and a secretary, and raised their children with a strong work ethic and traditional Christian values. Coming from a 1950's style mainline Christian tradition, my folks prayed at the dinner table and bedtime, obliged the family to attend worship services on Sunday, volunteered at the church and tried to live a good life during the other six days of the week. While a prayer vigil, Bible study or praying for our unsaved friends and neighbors were all foreign concepts to our family, the obligatory church attendance, my first Sunday school teacher, and our Baptist neighbor would all play critical roles in my story down the road.

Unlike most missionaries, I did not sense my calling in childhood. Despite making a decision to receive Jesus Christ as my Savior at age 7, during a backyard bible club hosted by my neighbor, my adolescent and teen years were marked by rebellion, partying and the pursuit of all sorts of worldly pleasures. My rebellion was so full blown that I once considered converting to Rastafarianism. Imagine my dismay when I discovered that religions' generally low opinion of Caucasians! Even after returning to the Lord as a young adult I was not particularly "mission minded" and certainly not children's ministry minded. In fact I had never actually met, prayed for or supported a missionary directly up until the time that GOD shook me from my slumber. I could only describe myself as unprepared, unqualified and unaware. Frankly, I was just thrilled to be on GOD's team, but I was clearly not varsity material.

Why the self-deprecation you ask? To begin with, whenever we take the audacious step of writing anything about our GOD, His Word, His Church or His purposes in this world, we need to do so with great humbleness of heart. I don't feel qualified to write this book, but what GOD has done in me has been so all-consuming, the message so critical, and

CHAPTER 1 – TURNING ONE HEART TO THE CHILDREN

the need so great, that I cannot ignore it. I cannot help but shout it from the rooftops. Isn't that what GOD asks of us? "You must go to everyone I send you to and say whatever I command you" Jeremiah 1:7. I want to tell my story because I wasn't in the fight and now I am. It is my hope that, by reading this, GOD might draw you into the battle as well. The Lord knows we need reinforcements.

My second motive for beginning with a word about my generally un-extraordinary beginnings is to encourage any of you who might think that GOD cannot use you or that you don't have anything special to offer. The fact is that, apart from our heavenly Father, none of us has anything special to offer. I am no different from you. I am certain that many, if not most, of you are more gifted, talented and experienced than I. But GOD in his wisdom chose the foolish and the weak. It is in that spirit that I begin my story, not because I am humble and don't want to take the credit, but because I, in fact, deserve none of the credit. I pray that in my story you might find similarities to your own and encouragement that GOD will move in your life as well, if you will just let him. I want you to come away saying, "If God can do that in **this** guy's life…"

"Now to him who is able to do immeasurably more than all we ask or imagine, according to his power that is at work within us, to him be glory in the church and in Christ Jesus throughout all generations, for ever and ever! Amen." Ephesians 3:20-21

Be Careful What You Pray For

It was 2000 and the year of my first "great awakening." As with most important spiritual revivals, this one began in the showroom of a car dealership in Northern Virginia. Well as unromantic as that sounds, it is the truth. At the time I was approaching thirty years of age. I had been walking with the Lord consistently for some ten years but had begun feeling like I had reached a spiritual plateau. I was attending a strong, Bible teaching church in Reston, Virginia with my wife and two young sons, had worked my way up through the corporate ranks to become Divisional Operations Manager in a Fortune 500 company and was, for the first time in our family's life, financially stable. Life was good but something was missing. I'd lost my fire for the Lord.

Put me in coach

Around that time someone challenged me with this idea; "Since Jesus began his earthly mission around age thirty, this is a critical age in every man's spiritual life." This thought created a pressure and uneasiness in my heart I had never experienced before. So as I sat in that showroom, waiting for my mother to complete the purchase of her new car, I shared my feelings with my brother-in-law, Joel. It went something like this. "You know, I feel like I'm back in High School football again. You know that feeling like you're on the sidelines; you're all geared up, but so far you're just watching the game? You're standing there next to the coach and you just want to say, "Put me in coach." "I feel like I'm spiritually out of the game and I want to play." Now, my brother-in-law is a certifiable goofball, one of the things I love most about him, but he is also a godly man who believes very strongly in the power of prayer and wastes no time in jumping right to it. "Let's pray for that right now!" And so we did. Right there in that showroom we bowed our heads together and prayed to the heavenly head coach that He would "put me in the game." Not exactly as beautiful as, "Here I am, send me" but GOD came through nevertheless.

Serve to Seek

My "Coach" wasted no time in getting to work on me, and He began with a lesson. Over the ensuing months I came to understand, for the first time, something that revolutionized my spiritual life; a truth critical to "getting in the game."

Seeking radically requires serving selflessly

Are you committed to radically seeking GOD's will? You need to level with yourself on some basic questions. Have I ever honestly said to GOD, "Here I am, send me" and really meant it? Have I ever genuinely said to GOD, "I am going to seek your face in your Word and in prayer and I will obey your Will no matter what I find there"? Have I followed through on my declaration?

That is radical seeking. You might say, "Declarations like that are just words. They don't mean anything." I would say that you are half right. Yes they are just words, but words spoken by a child of GOD in the name of Jesus are powerful. Remember GOD "spoke" the universe into existence. Jesus said, "If you have faith as small as a mustard seed, you can *say* to this mountain, 'Move from here to there,' and it will move. Nothing will be impossible for you." Paul wrote in Romans 10:9, "If you **declare with your mouth**, "Jesus is Lord," and believe in your heart that God raised him from the dead, you will be saved." Words have power and it is important that we declare our intentions to the Lord, pledge our allegiance, and then follow through.

Seekers are finders

So if we must be faithful, radical seekers of GOD's will, we need to know what constitutes really effective seeking. Effective seeking, results in finding. That seems elementary but if you seek and never find, you are being "ineffective." Clearly effective seeking involves prayer and meditation on GOD's Word. Going to any other fount for truth is not only ineffective but also dangerous. But is hearing from GOD enough? Jesus said, "But everyone who **hears** these words of mine and does not put them into practice is like a foolish man who built his house on the sand." So effective seeking requires action, it involves selfless service. Have you met people who say they aren't serving because they are waiting

CHAPTER 1 – TURNING ONE HEART TO THE CHILDREN

for GOD to reveal His "will" for their life? They are just not sure where GOD wants them to serve. They are "seeking" His will presumably by sitting at home waiting for a voice from the clouds. Perhaps that person is you. Well let me share something simple that one of my mentors once shared with me. It is simple, but its impact on my relationship with GOD and his Word were profound. GOD's "will" for our lives is clearly laid out in scripture in hundreds of places like,

Micah 6:8,

"He has shown you, O mortal, what is good.

And what does the LORD require of you?

To act justly and to love mercy

and to walk humbly with your GOD",

1 Peter 4:10

"Each of you should use whatever gift you have received to serve others, as faithful stewards of GOD's grace in its various forms."

LAST MAN STANDING

Galatians 5:13

"You, my brothers and sisters, were called to be free. But do not use your freedom to indulge the flesh; rather, serve one another humbly in love."

James 1:27

"Religion that GOD our Father accepts as pure and faultless is this: to look after orphans and widows in their distress and to keep oneself from being polluted by the world."

Mark 12:30 and 31

"Love the Lord your GOD with all your heart and with all your soul and with all your mind and with all your strength.' 31 The second is this: 'Love your neighbor as yourself.' There is no commandment greater than these."

Matthew 28:19

"Therefore go and make disciples of all nations, baptizing them in the name of the Father and of the Son and of the Holy Spirit,"

That's it friend. GOD's written, revealed will for all of his children is clearly laid out in scripture. What are we waiting for? Of course we would know this if we were earnestly and honestly, or "radically," seeking the Lord with a

CHAPTER 1 – TURNING ONE HEART TO THE CHILDREN

heart surrendered and willing to do whatever is asked or required of us. It's as plain as day for anyone with ears to hear.

GOD's <u>hidden</u> will, things like who will I marry, where will I go to college and what job should I take, He will reveal along the way as we follow Him in obedience. GOD's Word is a "lamp to my feet" not a flood light on my future. God is not going to give you a 5 or 10-year plan with charts and graphs. He desires that his children simply obey in the small things, showing they are "faithful in little" so that he can show them greater things. Serving is a critical component of seeking GOD's calling on our lives. If we want to see GOD open doors and make our "paths straight," we need to go ahead and start taking the first steps of faith with the information we have already revealed to us in scripture.

So that is what I determined to do. The months following my car dealership awakening were a flurry of activity as GOD presented opportunities for me to teach a 6th grade boys Sunday school class (where I discovered that I love teaching and writing curriculum), to teach English as a Second Language alongside my wife (where I discovered a love for people from other lands), to form a home bible study (where I met people who would play critical roles in our early ministry years) and to run the coffee shop ministry for a new worship service at our church (where I learned that sometimes service isn't glamorous but you "gotta do what you gotta do"). In and through all of these opportunities GOD was working in my life and preparing my heart for something new.

Compassion

In December of 2000 my wife, Patricia, and I travelled to Brazil with our two boys to visit her family over the holidays as we had many times since we married in 1995. It just so happened that I was spending my devotional time on the compassion of Jesus in Matthew 9:36. Scripture tells us that as Jesus went from village to village and encountered the people living there, "he had **compassion** on them, because they were harassed and helpless." As we left the airport in the mega-city of São Paulo, and made the journey past the shantytowns, past the homeless living beneath every overpass and children begging on the street corners, something hit me and hit me hard. Beyond the purely intellectual acknowledgement that this reality was "unfortunate" and sad at some superficial level, I felt absolutely no emotion, no compassion and certainly no strong desire to do anything about it. How could this be? "I am a Christian", I thought, "a follower of the most compassionate One and yet I am an emotional flat line." The uneasiness in my heart that had preceded my first spiritual awakening was back.

The road trip that changed everything

One afternoon during our visit, my father-in-law asked if I would accompany him the following morning back to São Paulo to retrieve his brother, Roberto, who was there receiving a cancer treatment. The city of São Paulo is one of the five largest cities in the world and is about a five-hour drive from

CHAPTER 1 – TURNING ONE HEART TO THE CHILDREN

the city of Assis, a town of about 100,000 souls, where my wife was born and raised. Knowing that the drive alone would be tedious for him, I agreed and, in order to get a good night of sleep before the drive, slept in a room apart from the one Patricia and our boys stayed in.

I still hadn't been able to shake that unsettled feeling about my compassion deficit. Remembering that Jesus said; "Until now you have not asked for anything in my name. Ask and you will receive, and your joy will be complete," (John 16:24) I decided to take advantage of the solitude and carry my need for compassion before the Lord in prayer.

Now I will preface the following account with the caveat that I am a typically cautious person when presented with the spiritual "experiences" of others. I tend to view goose bumps, warm feelings and vague "leadings from the Lord" with a good dose of skepticism. After all, our emotions, fatigue, expectations and even our diet can play tricks on our minds. On this occasion I chose to pray lying face down on the bed. As I prayed, very sincerely asking GOD to resurrect that part of His image in me that is compassionate, a warm feeling began to pass over my body from my head down, not unlike the feeling one gets when receiving a strong pain killer intravenously. This comforting warmth was accompanied by a brightness within my closed eyes as though someone were shining a flashlight in my face even though my face was down on the pillow. As odd as all this seemed I didn't have time to process any of it as I slipped off to sleep almost immediately.

Answered Prayer

The following morning I awoke with not so much as a second thought about the previous night's experience and headed off for the long drive. After picking up Uncle Roberto at the cancer hospital, we began to navigate our way back out of the city, my father-in-law, Rubens, at the wheel and I riding shotgun. That is when it happened; something so small and yet it literally redirected the course of my life. We stopped at one of the thousands of traffic lights in this sprawling metropolis. We were about five cars back from the front. As we waited in the stifling heat for the signal to change, I noticed a boy, probably seven or eight year's old, barefoot and dirty, with the ragged t-shirt and shorts combo typical of street kids in South America. He was going from car to car, knocking on each window and extending his grubby hand for some change. I couldn't take my eyes off of him. I was mesmerized. As he moved his way back, finally arriving on the driver's side of our car, something miraculous happened. This boy, whose name I will never know, didn't knock at our window. Unlike at every other car, he didn't extend his hand. Instead, he looked through the window, past my father-in-law and directly into my eyes. Those sad, deep brown eyes seemed to be pouring into my soul all the sorrow and suffering of his story.

At that moment, as we looked into each other's eyes for what seemed like an eternity, I heard GOD's voice speaking to my heart, "You asked for my compassion, well here it is." The feeling that washed over me can only be described as melting or perhaps a dam rupturing and releasing its power all at once on the valley below. I could suddenly understand what the Lord meant when he said he would remove my heart of stone and replace it with a heart of flesh (Ezekiel 36:26). GOD's resurrection power had done something amazing in that instant. I suddenly felt deep sadness and a real desire to do something even though I had no idea what. As the light turned green and we moved away I turned my head toward the window and wept quietly. Even then I didn't realize what a game changing answer to prayer that really was, but it would all become clearer soon.

On Fire

Arriving back in Assis I was on fire. I wanted to take every street-kid into the house, make them lunch and share Christ with them (even though I didn't speak much Portuguese at the time). My mind was going a million miles per hour. This compassion thing had opened up a whole new world to me. The fire continued blazing and my mind reeling after we returned home to Virginia. Along with that flame came a real burden for the spiritual and physical needs of children, particularly children in Brazil. From that burden a vision began to take shape in my mind. The vision was of a Christ centered community outreach that would minister to at-risk children. It would be a place where they could be kids;

a safe place where they could see, hear and experience the love of Christ and find the narrow path that leads to abundant life, just as I had found way back in my neighbors' backyard bible club. It would begin in Assis.

Despite all the excitement there were some very real hurdles to clear. For one, I hadn't shared this grand plan with Patricia yet. This was largely because we had just purchased our first home, a longtime dream of ours, and we were getting ready to move in. I, being the brave, macho man that I am, was absolutely terrified at what her reaction might be to my news and the possible implications for our "comfortable" life. The other thing holding me back was that, being a big shot Operations Manager gave me exactly zero experience with Christian missions, much less working with at-risk children. I could imagine the looks of doubt I would get from my family, friends, colleagues and church leaders were I to share my big idea.

Moving Day

With the last of our worldly possessions loaded into the back of a little box truck, we rolled through Loudoun county Virginia on our way to our first home, a neat little end unit townhouse in Ashburn. Everything we'd ever wanted. Patricia's joy was almost palpable as we turned into the quaint little community of Ashburn Village. Always a master of timing, I decided that this was the moment for true confessions. "So sweetie, I have a hypothetical question for

CHAPTER 1 – TURNING ONE HEART TO THE CHILDREN

you," I said, thinking that would throw her off. "What would you say if I told you that I felt the Lord calling us to go to Brazil to minister to at-risk children?" Brave no? Smooth certainly? Well she started to cry. I kid you not. I made her cry. What was I thinking!? This was going to be bad. And then she spoke. "I have been feeling GOD say the same thing to me for a long time now and I was just afraid to say anything to you, what with us buying our dream home and all. I thought you'd think I was crazy." O me of little faith. GOD had this all worked out ahead of time. Why had I had doubts? What kind of missionary has doubts?

Doubts

Now what do we do? Sell it all and book our tickets to Brazil? Not so fast. Even with that confirmation from the Lord there was still the reality of our total lack of qualifications and the financial resources necessary to begin a ministry. Aside from a few months of experience as a Sunday school and ESL teacher, I had no training and no experience. How could we hope to begin? Are you sure you want us in **this** game Coach? I felt like a Junior Varsity player asking to play in the Super Bowl. The Lord used two examples from scripture to minister to my heart in those days and to shine a little light on what He had in mind. The first is this passage from the book of the prophet Amos.

LAST MAN STANDING

"Amos answered Amaziah, "I was neither a prophet nor a prophet's son, but I was a shepherd, and I also took care of sycamore-fig trees. But the Lord took me from tending the flock and said to me, 'Go, prophesy to my people Israel." Amos 7:14-15

GOD has a record of taking people completely out of their comfort zone to do His work. No matter what we think our giftedness is, GOD knows us better. This way there is little doubt as to who is worthy of the glory and the praise. It is always the Caller and never the called. GOD was going to be able to use me. Though I couldn't see how, He who called would also prepare and empower.

The second example was of Moses and his eventual return to Egypt to lead GOD's people into freedom. You may recall that when Moses first sensed his "calling" he presumptuously moved out to respond, by killing an Egyptian, without waiting on GOD's direction and preparation (Exodus 2:11-15). It took forty years in the desert learning to protect and lead sheep, while under the spiritual tutelage of his father-in-law, the priest of Midian, before GOD had prepared and humbled Moses sufficiently to be the leader of the Exodus. Now I am no Moses to be certain, but the principle GOD seemed to be impressing on me was, don't be presumptuous. I will do this in My time. What could I say? "Here I am Lord, prepare me."

CHAPTER 1 – TURNING ONE HEART TO THE CHILDREN

Despite the obvious "giants in the land" (Numbers 13:32), we were convinced this burden was of GOD so we committed to prayer and told the Lord that we would obey and take the first small steps towards a life of full-time ministry and missionary service.

Passed Through Fire

The Lord went right to work. For starters, my career as an Operations Manager in the commercial real-estate field came to an abrupt end, due the downturn in the market following the terror attacks of September 11. Things got so bad that by March of 2002 our company had decided to sell our division off to a competitor. I had the uniquely distasteful experience of letting go a lot of very fine people and then letting myself go as well when I chose not to move to another division in Minnesota.

Jobless, with two small children, and a mortgage to pay I was struggling to see what part this could possibly have in His plan. The only work I could find quickly was with an automobile dealership. Again with the car dealership! And again my brother-in-law Joel was there with an "encouraging" take on the situation. "Working on pure commission will certainly be the closest thing to living by faith that you've ever done." Thanks a lot! But you know what, that stint as a car salesman did teach me some critical lessons in faith. Besides getting great deals for every family member and friend I could think of, I made almost no money as a car salesman. To put it simply, I was horrible. But I did discover that, despite my failings, GOD is still faithful. Not once during those days did we miss a mortgage payment or go without food on our table. GOD provides. Lesson learned.

A short time later Patricia was, very uncharacteristically, thumbing through one of those community newspapers that no one ever reads, when she saw an ad for an Operations Manager at a nearby community center. "Hmm", we thought; "a community center." "That seems to fit with our vision for ministry. Sounds like it might be a GOD thing, let's check it out." When I went in for the interview it really did seem like a "GOD thing." The management team was made up mostly of other Christians and the position involved overseeing all of Operations including children's programming. This would give me my first opportunity to gain experience that I would need developing community based programs in Brazil. It sounded perfect. I was called in for a second interview and offered the job.

Perfect, right? My heart sunk when they told me the salary, half of what I had been making in my previous management position. How could I take a job that I knew wouldn't be enough to pay the bills? At least selling cars I could *potentially* make enough, even though that never happened. I went home to talk with Patricia. We prayed, we talked and we prayed some more. When we came back to talk again we both felt that this was in fact a GOD thing and that we would need to trust Him again. I served happily as the

Operations Manager of that little community center for a year. And you know what? We never missed a payment or went hungry. One month Patricia told me over dinner that we didn't have enough to pay the mortgage that was coming due. We prayed and, what do you know, we received a check from the IRS for a tax refund we didn't know we were getting. It was just enough to pay the bills. Over and over again that year GOD showed Himself strong on our behalf and strengthened our faith.

> *"Don't worry, because your Father in heaven knows that you need all these things." Matthew 6:32*

Equipped by the church

At the same time that we were being given practical training in faith-based ministry, we began a mission's internship program through our church, Reston Bible Church. Back when we first felt the call to missions I had contacted the chairman of the Reston Bible missions committee to ask his advice. He didn't know me from Adam but graciously invited me out to breakfast and then patiently listened to my whole story. I'm not sure what he thought of me there tearfully telling him how I was going to follow GOD's call to Brazil, but I do know that he gave me some very good advice. Hold your horses! Draw close to your home church, he said. It is the church's role to prepare, anoint and send missionaries into the world. If you go off half-cocked you are likely to cause more damage to yourself, your family and your cause than good.

This brother is a tough ex-police officer who shoots straight and pulls no punches. I would love to say that my relationship with him and our missions' leadership has always been lots of holding hands and kumbaya, but the reality is that we had our share of conflicts and misunderstandings in the beginning. My wiring has always led me to question the way things are done if it doesn't make sense to me and to push the limits of change. In the business world my "wiring" was an asset, but I'm afraid it rocked the boat a bit in "church world." As you might imagine I probably gave church leadership more than a few grey hairs. In the end and through it all Patricia and I learned a tremendous amount about godly authority and leadership. The internship program gave us an invaluable base of knowledge in missiology, the history of Christian missions, the role of the church and the width and breadth of the modern missions' movement. For this we owe an enormous debt of gratitude to the faithful members of the Reston Bible Church Missions' Committee for lovingly holding the reins on this zealot and giving us godly direction. To this day our sending church is an enormous source of blessing and encouragement in our lives as they are to the hundreds of missionaries they support around the world.

CHAPTER 1 – TURNING ONE HEART TO THE CHILDREN

Field Tested

In early 2003 Patricia and I led a team from several northern Virginia churches down to Brazil on a "scouting" mission and to hold an evangelistic day camp. We had made contact with a local church that was interested in impacting the children there and were hopeful that they would become an ongoing partner. The mission, which led to a follow up trip in 2004, was a huge success and served to confirm even more clearly to us that this was where we were supposed to be.

At the end of that first mission the senior Pastor there in Brazil sat us down and asked point blank if we would come and stay full time to help them continue the work. I can't explain why, maybe it was the caution I had learned with our missions committee, but I politely told him that, yes, it was our heart's desire to come and stay someday, but that we would need to pray about it and let him know if GOD confirmed the timing. I couldn't believe my own restraint, but I was sure that when the time was right GOD would make it very clear. One of the folks on that first team was also, at the time, the coordinator for the Children's Ministry at our home church. Upon returning to Virginia from Brazil that year, she asked if I would be interested in leading a soccer camp outreach that the church had planned for that spring. Still "seeking through serving," I accepted immediately. What I didn't know was that she had also put a bug in the ear of the interim Director of Children's Ministries that I might be someone to look at in their search for a new Director.

The Next Big Step

At the end of camp I gave them both a briefing on how things had gone and what changes I would make in future outreaches. As I wrapped up my report she looked at me thoughtfully for a moment and then, as if someone had spoken a word of confirmation into her ear, she asked, "Have you ever considered becoming a children's pastor?" "Why yes, I have been preparing for doing evangelism and discipleship with at-risk children in Brazil," I responded. She said, "No, I mean here at the church. We need a man whose heart beats for children's ministry to come on full-time." Another curve ball we didn't see coming. Again Patricia and I prayed, we talked and we prayed some more but it was difficult to imagine a more perfect next step in preparing for the mission field. So, in the summer of 2003, I was offered the opportunity of a lifetime as the Children's Ministry Director for Reston Bible Church in Reston, Virginia.

From 2003 to 2006 we were blessed and honored to minister to the children and families of RBC, teach GOD's Word, write curriculum, shepherd a volunteer staff of nearly 200 adults, and develop relationships with brothers and sisters in Christ that will last a lifetime. I had the opportunity to study and sit under godly teaching that would begin to develop what has become my life message, and the basis for this book. As you can see, by "serving to seek" we found in every one of these opportunities, and challenges, a door that GOD opened in preparing us for the work He had called us to.

CHAPTER 1 – TURNING ONE HEART TO THE CHILDREN

Go Time

In early 2005 we traveled back to Brazil. As I sat one afternoon with a Pastor and friend, who we had met on our previous mission projects in Assis, sipping afternoon coffee, he began to layout for me a burden and vision that he felt GOD was impressing on him. It was a little like the twilight zone. I had never shared our long-term vision with this Pastor before, but as he talked I heard him describing in great detail the very thing GOD had placed on our hearts years earlier. He ended by saying, "The church wants to get behind this, but we need someone to lead. I realize that you have a home, a family and a thriving ministry but…could you be that person?" Once I got over my goose bumps, I told him that we would pray over it and get back to him. It was the opportunity we had dreamed about and our prayers and conversations confirmed it was time. It had been a wild ride, but the Lord had brought us through five years of preparation and now "Open Arms Brazil," or "Braços Abertos Brasil," as the ministry is known in Portuguese, would be born. We had so much more to learn but that would come as we continued to be refined by both trial and triumph.

Don't Miss Out on Your Story

I wanted to share a little of how GOD turned my heart to the children because, if you count yourself a disciple of

Jesus Christ and have been feeling a little "out of the game," then I want to encourage you. The Christian life is so much more than salvation. It is abundant life in this world, adventure, brotherhood, joy, peace and eternal purpose. All of this is only possible when you are in the game.

Let's imagine that you have been selected to be part of your favorite sports team. You didn't deserve to make the squad but someone powerful, as an act of grace, gave you the great honor to wear the uniform. You might say this would never happen. That is true. It would be a miracle, just as it is a miracle that the God of the Universe would give us sinners the right to become His children. You are thankful and proud of course, but you never show up for the orientation or workouts. You don't hang out at the training table with the other players on the team. In fact you never really ask about those things at all. Maybe no one told you about them. Maybe you didn't have time. Or maybe you felt like you didn't really deserve to be part of the team at all. Then your teammates head off to play your greatest rival and win a hard fought game. They win big! Upon their return there are stories of big plays, of camaraderie, of glory, of sacrifice and triumph. You heard there was a game but figured it was not for you. After all, you hadn't been to a single workout. Now there you are. You have the uniform, your name is on the roster, but you have slept through the best part of being part of this championship team. If you are not going to take the field, then what's the point?

CHAPTER 1 – TURNING ONE HEART TO THE CHILDREN

Don't let this happen to you Christian. Don't miss out on the banquet that is the Christian life because you thought it was just about admittance to a heavenly feast down the road. This is not a book to guilt you into international missions. That was my calling, but probably not yours. This is a call to step up and get in the battle where you are. Serve to seek and GOD **will** honor you.

Get it done – What is this "Good News?"

For those of you that are asking, "What in the world are you talking about? What's with all this "calling" and "Jesus" stuff?" I am glad you picked up this book. It wasn't an accident. Let me explain.

Have you ever felt like there is no GOD and that you are just battling alone with your own human desires and your conscience and can't ever seem to get it right? Have you wondered why the things that you sense in your heart are right you can't seem to do with consistency and yet the things you know are wrong come so easily? Have you ever felt like there is an empty space inside that you can't seem to fill or that you can't seem to find your purpose? Do you feel alone and disconnected in the universe? Well the sad truth is that you ARE alone and disconnected and without hope. This is bad news.

Thankfully that is not how it was meant to be. The truth is that there is a GOD and He created you and loves you and wants to do amazing things in and through your life. He wants you on his team. Unfortunately our connection to him has been severed by our stubborn lack of faith and obedience to his commands. GOD's word says that, "all have sinned and fallen short of the glory of GOD," and also that, "the wages of sin is death." God wants us to be glorious as He is glorious. Anything less is not acceptable. Sin is everything we do, say, think, or don't do, say or think that doesn't conform to GOD's perfect will for us. Because GOD is perfectly just he must punish sin. The punishment for sin is the absence of GOD's presence in our lives now and for all eternity in a place called hell. That's death in the physical and spiritual sense. That is justice.

But GOD is also love, and to reconcile his love and his justice he chose to send his Son to live as a human but without sin, a sinless man that would give himself as the ultimate sacrifice to pay the penalty for the sins of mankind. Because we all sit under the same death sentence, only Jesus, the sinless man, was qualified to pay the price for us. A debt he didn't owe. He defeated death and the grave, a historical fact, and stands offering redemption and forgiveness, a reconnection with GOD's presence, if we only accept it. Jesus is the last man standing for you and for me. The Bible says in Romans 10:9 that,

"If you declare with your mouth, "Jesus is Lord," and believe in your heart that GOD raised him from the dead, you will be saved. For it is with your heart that you believe and are justified, and it is with your mouth that you profess your faith and are saved."

CHAPTER 1 – TURNING ONE HEART TO THE CHILDREN

No amount of good work you do can earn your way in. Your good won't outweigh your bad. Sorry, but that's just not how justice works. How many judges would drop charges against you just because you're a nice guy and you've done all kinds of charity work?

This is a crossroads moment. It is a choice you need to make and I can assure you it will only be the beginning of a great adventure. So if you feel GOD speaking to you, I suggest you answer now. Get it done. As they say in the old westerns I love so much, "It's time to make amends with your Maker." If you have believed in your heart that Jesus is the living Son of GOD who died for your sins, and have confessed publicly with your mouth that Jesus is Lord of your life, then welcome to the family. If you are not convinced I would like to challenge you to find a Bible and just read through the gospel of John. No strings attached. I think it might just change your life.

So that is my story. Are you ready to begin writing your own? There is a world of children who are waiting for the answer.

Let's take a moment to pray as we begin your journey,

"Father in heaven, creator and sustainer of the universe, we humbly come before you and ask that you would apply your resurrection power to those areas of our lives that are yet to be touched and transformed into the image of your Son Jesus. Turn our hearts to the children we pray. Amen."

Chapter 2 - What GOD knows, Satan exploits, and the church has forgotten

"Train up a child in the way he should go,

And when he is old he will not depart from it." Proverbs 22:6

CHAPTER 2 – WHAT GOD KNOWS, SATAN EXPLOITS AND THE CHURCH HAS FORGOTTEN

There is something essential about human beings as children that the Creator knows. It is plain to see throughout His revealed Word. Children are precious and they must be reached and taught GOD's truth when they are young. Our adversary, Satan, understands this full well, as is evident by even a superficial survey of his attempts at misleading children. Sadly, much of the Church has forgotten this essential truth and we have either dumbed down our approach or gone AWOL in executing our responsibilities. As the "last man standing" in this fight we must shake off our punch drunk haze and refocus on the task at hand.

What GOD Knows

Ever wonder what was first on GOD's list of priorities as he established his people Israel? Before they ever even got out of Egypt? The children. What was the very first ceremony GOD chose to ordain? The Passover. It is this ceremony that would characterize the Jewish people for centuries and point to our celebration of the Lord's Supper in the new covenant. And what was the purpose of this ceremony? Let's go to the source.

> *Then Moses summoned all the elders of Israel and said to them, "Go at once and select the animals for*

your families and slaughter the Passover lamb. Take a bunch of hyssop, dip it into the blood in the basin and put some of the blood on the top and on both sides of the doorframe. None of you shall go out of the door of your house until morning. When the LORD goes through the land to strike down the Egyptians, he will see the blood on the top and sides of the doorframe and will pass over that doorway, and he will not permit the destroyer to enter your houses and strike you down. "Obey these instructions as a lasting ordinance for you and your descendants. **When you enter the land that the LORD will give you as he promised, observe this ceremony.** <u>**And when your children ask you,**</u> **'What does this ceremony mean to you?' then tell them,** *'It is the Passover sacrifice to the LORD, who passed over the houses of the Israelites in Egypt and spared our homes when he struck down the Egyptians.'" Then the people bowed down and worshiped. The Israelites did just what the LORD commanded Moses and Aaron.*

Exodus 12:21-28 NIV (emphasis added)

In establishing the Passover festival GOD provided the Israelites their first children's ministry tool! Many years ago, after participating in a Passover Seder (a Hebrew word which means "order" or "arrangement") hosted by my sister, Lynn, and brother-in-law Joel, a Jewish Christian, Patricia and I decided to bring that tradition into our family as well. We have celebrated a Christian form of the Seder every year since.

CHAPTER 2 – WHAT GOD KNOWS, SATAN EXPLOITS AND THE CHURCH HAS FORGOTTEN

The ceremony is a beautiful act of worship, rich with scripture and symbols that bring the relationship between the Jewish exodus from Egypt and the sacrifice of Christ, the Lamb of GOD who takes away the sin of the world, into bright focus.

More than anything else the thing that struck me about this several hours' long ceremony is the important place that is given to the children. Rather than removing the children to play games, watch a movie or color, they have a critical role to play in the meal. The Haggadah itself, the liturgical text or script for the ceremony, was derived from the scriptures in direct response to the command to, "tell your children." It begins with the children searching the house for any "leaven", a symbol for sin, so that it can be removed and the ceremony commenced. The children ask the questions that lead us through the story of the first Passover. Questions like, "Why is this night different from all other nights?" From beginning to end the Passover ceremony is an interactive object lesson, bringing adults and children together to learn, remember and worship the living GOD who "passed over" our sins to bring us into communion with Him.

GOD placed such an emphasis on reaching and teaching children His ways, that his prologue to the commands for the generation of Israelites that would enter the Promised Land in Deuteronomy includes this warning,

"Only be careful, and watch yourselves closely so that you do not forget the things your eyes have seen or let them fade from your heart

as long as you live. ***Teach them to your children and to their children after them.*** *Remember the day you stood before the LORD your GOD at Horeb, when he said to me, "Assemble the people before me to hear my words so that they may learn to revere me as long as they live in the land* ***and may teach them to their children.****" Deuteronomy 4:9-10 (emphasis added)*

Throughout Deuteronomy there are admonitions to teach the children. These are not mere Bible stories either, but deep discussions of faith and doctrine.

"Impress them on your children. Talk about them when you sit at home and when you walk along the road, when you lie down and when you get up." Deuteronomy 6:7

Notice the strength of the words employed. "**Impress** them on your children." "Talk (discuss) about them." Children should be encouraged, at all ages, to discuss doctrine, scripture and their thoughts about the Lord.

So critical was the teaching of children to GOD's plan that it played a significant part in His choosing of Abraham as the father of this new people. In Genesis 18:17-19 we read, "And the LORD said, "Shall I hide from Abraham that thing which I do, seeing that Abraham shall surely become a great and mighty nation, and all the nations of the earth shall be blessed in him? **For I know him, that he will command his children** and his household after him, and they shall keep the way of the LORD to do justice and judgment, that the LORD may bring upon Abraham that which He hath spoken of him."

CHAPTER 2 – WHAT GOD KNOWS, SATAN EXPLOITS AND THE CHURCH HAS FORGOTTEN

GOD knew the character of the man he had chosen and a vital trait was his commitment to command (teach) his children.

Was this merely an Old Testament theme? Not at all. Let's look at that famous scene where the disciples are trying to keep the children away from the Master. I like to imagine Peter acting like a well-meaning, but uptight usher on Sunday morning shushing the little ones and advising the parents that they need to take them to "Sunday School", usually in some out of the way place where their noise won't interrupt the really important work of adult ministry. But Jesus wasn't having any of it. He reprimanded the disciples and then took them to school.

"Then people brought little children to Jesus for him to place his hands on them and pray for them. But the disciples rebuked them.

Jesus said, "Let the little children come to me, and do not hinder them, for the kingdom of heaven belongs to such as these." Matthew 9:13-14

So what is it that GOD knows about children that causes him to place such an emphasis on them? Well for one, GOD has a soft spot for those unable to defend themselves; those groups of people in society who depend on the grace of others in order to survive and thrive. That is clear throughout scripture and particularly in the Old Testament laws governing Jewish civil society. But His focus on children goes beyond protection and provision. ***To put it simply the Creator knows that if you, "train up a child in the way he should go"*** *(according to how GOD has wired that child), "even when he is old he will not depart from it." (Proverbs 22:6).*

I can hear the objections now. "My cousin so and so grew up in a Christian home and he's an ax murderer now." To which I would say, like most proverbs, this one is a principle, not a hard and fast rule. That being said, it has been my experience that children who are raised by committed, equipped and engaged Christian parents, continue on that path and do not turn from it. Notice I said, raised by **committed, equipped and engaged** Christian parents. Just being "Christian" parents doesn't cut it. Let me take a moment to color in the picture.

Committed – "Never give up!"

A committed parent recognizes their central role as spiritual leader of their child. This parent seeks knowledge and understanding regarding the raising of their child. A committed parent invites other godly role models into their child's life in order to compensate for their own weak areas and give their child the best shot at hope and a future. These parents know it is going to be hard, but they take Winston Churchill's advice to heart and "never, never, never, give up" on their kids, even in the late rounds, those dark hours when their teenager hates them and thinks they are ruining her life.

CHAPTER 2 – WHAT GOD KNOWS, SATAN EXPLOITS AND THE CHURCH HAS FORGOTTEN

Equipped – "Geared up with God's Word"

Parents who belong to a church that excels at its biblical mandate to equip the saints for works of service, and understands that one of the greatest works we have to complete is that of raising a generation that knows and loves the Lord, will tend to be better equipped to take on the task. Those who are not blessed with a church family like that, but are committed to their calling, have found the wealth of excellent material for every parenting style, personality type and gifting imaginable, and taken advantage of it. These parents have sought out and applied GOD's wisdom as found in scripture. They are geared up for the battle.

Engaged – "Win their hearts with love"

Josh McDowell has said, "Truth without relationship leads to rejection." [1] A parent, who is committed to their child and equipped with good information, may still fail at raising up that child in the way that he should go. We must engage our children in loving and safe relationships if we want to be heard. Parents who are engaged seek out ways to live out their faith before their children. These parents are interested in quantity as well as quality time. An engaged parent moves toward their child, even when that child's world seems

---

[1] Josh McDowell Ministry, "Relationships that Transform"

strange or uninteresting to them. They follow the example of our heavenly Father who, in order to reconcile his creation to himself, moved toward us on His own by sending his only Son. An engaged parent makes unconditional sacrifices to win the heart of their child.

> *"Raise up a child in the way he should go"*

And what of the child who strays?

Beyond affirming the veracity of Proverbs 22:6, I would even dare to say that every child who is raised in a genuinely Christian home and still strays from their faith as a teen or adult, lives in utter spiritual conflict, knowing full well that they have turned their back on the Truth. It is also true that children with a Christian family background like the one I described above stand a much better chance of returning to the Lord than those who never heard the name of Jesus in their childhood. Why I am so confident? I was one of them. I understood the Gospel and my condition as a sinner before a holy GOD and prayed to receive Christ at age seven. I grew up in a church that, while not particularly evangelistic, did do a reasonably good job of teaching us the broad strokes of GOD's story of redemption. When I fell to the temptations of youth and rebelled it was not with a clear conscience, as was the case with most of my friends at the time. I didn't wake up one morning and decide I didn't believe in my heart that Jesus is the Son of GOD who died for my sins and laid claim to my life. No, I argued with Him, telling Him I wanted to enjoy

CHAPTER 2 – WHAT GOD KNOWS, SATAN EXPLOITS AND THE CHURCH HAS FORGOTTEN

"the pleasures of sin for a season." I argued with my older sister when she tried to call me back to the Lord (as she often reminds me, I actually launched a Bible at her and my brother-in-law during one particularly heated conversation). At every turn my conscience and the Holy Spirit convicted me. And yet I pushed ahead in rebellion for years until God finally brought this prodigal son fully to his knees in brokenness.

That's just one story you say. True enough, but statistics don't lie. **GOD knows that when you reach a child today you are in fact impacting generations to come.** George Barna's research, published in his ground breaking book, "Transforming Children into Spiritual Champions," confirmed what GOD said so succinctly in Proverbs 22:6. According to his studies, a person's worldview, their beliefs about life, faith, GOD, personal values, truth, integrity and the significance of the life, death and resurrection of Jesus Christ are fixed by age 14. Based on his findings, he wrote:

"Families, churches and para-church ministries must recognize that the primary window of opportunity for effectively reaching people with the good news of Jesus' death and resurrection is during the pre-teen years. It is during those years that people develop their frames of reference for the remainder of their life – especially theologically and morally. Consistently explaining and modeling truth principles for young people is the most critical factor in their spiritual development."[2]

Barna's research also showed that people from ages 5 through 13 have a 32% probability of accepting Christ as their savior. Young people from the ages of 14 through 18 have just a 4% likelihood of doing so, while adults (ages 19 through death) have only a 6% probability of making that choice.

Not only do children more readily accept the gospel, but they also remain stronger Christians throughout their lives. In his October 11, 2004 article titled, "Evangelism Is Most Effective Among Kids," Barna had this to say, "People who become Christian before their teen years are more likely than those who are converted when older to remain "absolutely committed" to Christianity." Try your own survey of adults you know who are working in full time Christian ministry and see how many became believers prior to the age of 13. My hunch is it will confirm Barna's work.

I once served as a camp counselor at a youth camp of a strong Bible teaching church filled with young people being raised in ostensibly Christian homes. These youth struggled and were tripped up by the same obstacles the world throws in front of un-churched youth. But something was different. Night after night youth stood to testify of how God had

---

[2] Barna Group, Transforming Children into Spiritual Champions, George Barna, Regal Books 2003.

CHAPTER 2 – WHAT GOD KNOWS, SATAN EXPLOITS AND THE CHURCH HAS FORGOTTEN

rescued them from everything from self-mutilation to drugs and alcohol. They strayed, they struggled, but something separated them from other children. These Christian young people belong to God by faith and as such are in the process of sanctification. They are not slaves to Satan's plans for them. They have dedicated Christian men and women around them, standing in the gap between them and this world system.

So I ask again, why am I so confident? First of all, because I believe that the Bible is GOD-breathed and completely trustworthy. So if GOD says that we need to teach the children, then we need to teach the children. It's really that simple. In addition to the commands to teach, scripture is chock full of examples of children and youth that GOD has used mightily in His plan of redemption. David, the prophet Jeremiah, Samuel, and Josiah to name a few. Then there is Paul's disciple, Timothy, of whom it was said, "From a child thou hast known the Holy Scriptures, which are able to make thee wise unto salvation through faith which is in Christ Jesus" (2 Timothy 3:15). And again we see in Psalm 8 that GOD ordains praises from the mouths of children and infants to establish a stronghold against his enemies.

Beyond that, if we should need further convincing, the statistical and anecdotal evidence bares this truth out over and over again in both the positive and the negative case, as we will look at next.

What Satan Exploits

Have you ever considered that the reverse of Proverbs 22:6 is also true? That if you raise up a child in the way that he should NOT go, even when he is old he will not depart from it?

Our enemy, Satan, is evil but he is no dummy. So if what I have laid out above about children were true we could expect to see him exploiting it for his own purposes. What kind of punches is he throwing at us? Where is he trying to hit hardest? At the risk of killing any future Presidential aspirations I might have, I'd like for us to consider just a few cases.

Influencing Education

Remember that old song from the play South Pacific, "You've Got to be Carefully Taught?" Catchy little tune and scarily true. Ask yourself, what is one of the key battlefields today for the struggle between traditional values and cultural relativism?

For decades in the arena of public education, atheistic groups and individuals, with their extreme left social agenda, have been fighting hard to do to our elementary schools what they succeeded in doing to our Universities. Where else could they have access to such a large, captive audience of children? Their dream scenario of course is that, with parents out of the way and mostly unaware of what is being taught, they would

CHAPTER 2 – WHAT GOD KNOWS, SATAN EXPLOITS AND THE CHURCH HAS FORGOTTEN

be free to preach their own "values neutral" doctrines that promote "ideals" like sexual permissiveness, deviance and disrespect for the role of parents, to name but a few examples. Why would our enemy be so bent on trying to influence education? If he can succeed in indoctrinating these children now he is practically guaranteed future adults sympathetic to his godless worldview.

The relative success of atheistic and statist organizations in influencing education, of course, varies from state to state and school to school depending on the leadership and teachers of that school, the community in which it is located, and the involvement of the parents in the education of their children.

Just to be crystal clear. This is not an indictment of public education or teachers. Neither am I saying we should all withdraw from public education: quite to the contrary. I am a product of public schools and my children have attended public school in Virginia. Thankfully there are still a great number of wonderful public schools staffed by dedicated teachers and administrators who struggle day in and day out because they love children. These individuals deserve our prayers and our support and certainly should not be condemned as part of the problem. They are on the front lines. If anything we should be encouraging more committed Jesus followers to enter the teaching profession from grade school right through the University level. The people of the Church must actively participate in local School Boards. While there are more educational options today, like home school and private Christian schools, public education is not an arena we can afford to withdraw from if we are to have any hope of leaving an intact civil society to our children.

Drug Gangs

The all-out assault on education would be bad enough, but our enemy doesn't limit himself to being a schoolyard bully. In many poor neighborhoods around the world children as young as five or six years of age are seduced, with candy, money or food for their family, by drug traffickers to work as lookouts and mules (couriers for illegal drug deliveries). They are often forced to experiment with their product. Getting them hooked young creates a customer base and cheap labor force for life. They are taught young to distrust and disrespect authority figures like police, teachers and often parents. The drug-gang is their family and the earlier they learn this lesson the more likely it will remain engraved on their psyche.

Pornography

Pornography is another market our enemy is strongly invested in. It is one of his greatest tools for destroying men, devaluing women and sexualizing children. I am reminded of that great Sunday school golden oldie, "O Be careful little eyes

CHAPTER 2 – WHAT GOD KNOWS, SATAN EXPLOITS AND THE CHURCH HAS FORGOTTEN

what you see" when I observe how across the world, porn magazines have left their former hiding places of shame, behind the counter or at least on the top shelf discretely covered, to their new prominence at eye level, not adult eye level mind you, but instead, for the average 8 year old child. It is no mistake that online porn purveyors work with pop-up ads for children's games like, "Click here to unlock thousands of FREE new games," that when clicked on, go directly to the most graphic content imaginable.

Satan knows full well the free access our children have to online information today and that, if you can addict the young mind to the chemical rush brought on by viewing pornography, you have hooked a customer for life and taken an enormous step towards delivering a knock-out punch to a future family or even contributing to a future rape or child molestation.

Media

No discussion of Satan's attack on children would be complete without mentioning the music industry and television media. Doubt it? Just consider the words of Bob Pittman, founder and former president of MTV. In an interview with Philadelphia Enquirer in 1982 Pittman said, "The strongest appeal you can make is emotionally. If you can get their emotions going, make them forget their logic, you've got them. At MTV, we don't shoot for the 14-year olds, **we**

own them!" (MTV is Rock Around the Clock, Philadelphia Inquirer, Nov. 3, 1982)

Satan knows that, just as music, a gift from GOD, is effective in carrying believers into deep emotional and Spirit-filled worship, it can, when twisted and distorted, effectively carry our children into dark places through lyrics that at once glorify violence, out-of-wedlock sex, and a hedonistic lifestyle, while at the same time belittling traditional values and virtues. The Black Eyed Peas, who I think have an enormous amount of talent, were recently the featured band on Nickelodeon's Kid's Choice Awards. In 2010, with their hit, "I gotta feeling," they were nominated for Favorite Song at these same awards. This song's lyrics, while promoting wild drinking and sex parties, are tame compared to the accompanying video clip that is essentially a look inside the rave party lifestyle, complete with bi-sexual quasi-orgy scenes and staggering drunks. Before I get accused of being a prude, remember folks, this was not the MTV awards, this was Nickelodeon's Kids Choice awards. The home of Sponge Bob Square Pants for goodness sake! Can there be any question that our children are the targets of an all-out informational and cultural attack?

No holds barred

As Jesus warns us in John's gospel, "the thief breaks in only to steal, kill and destroy." Sometimes he does it subtly. But if he can't get the children through more inconspicuous

CHAPTER 2 – WHAT GOD KNOWS, SATAN EXPLOITS AND THE CHURCH HAS FORGOTTEN

means there is always force. In spiritual warfare, just as in physical war, when diplomacy breaks down, you send in the door kickers. Satan does not shy away from this no-holds-barred approach. One glaring example is in Africa, the frontlines of the battle between Christianity and Radical Islam. In Nigeria and other African nations the kidnapping of Christian children by Muslim raiders is becoming increasingly common. These stolen children are forced to attend Muslim religious schools and convert to Islam. The following account was extracted from an article in Compass Direct News,

> "Victor Udo UsenSOKOTO, Nigeria, March 14 (Compass Direct News) – Beginning in November of last year, 13-year-old Victor Udo Usen, a member of the Christ Apostolic Church in this northern Nigeria city, went missing.
>
> On February 20, news that young Victor was spotted in a Muslim neighbor's house jolted his family. A young Christian girl had raced to the Usens' home in the Mabera area of Sokoto city with the news.
>
> Victor's mother, Esther Udo Usen, told Compass that she ran to the house where her son had been seen. She met him, however, even as he was making

frantic efforts to escape from the house where he has been held incommunicado for six months. "I quickly held his hands and dragged him along with me towards our house," she said. "But within a twinkle of an eye, I heard shouts of 'Allahu Akbar! Allahu Akbar! Allahu Akbar [GOD is great]!' I was shocked as I saw a large number of Muslims rushing towards us."

The mob surrounded them and snatched her son away from her, she told Compass with tears in her eyes. Before she could send for her husband, who was not home at the time, members of the mob told her that her son was now a Muslim and that she and her husband were no longer his parents."

The examples of Satan's targeted attacks on children go on and on. The apostle's warning in 1 Peter 5:8 to, "Be alert and of sober mind. Your enemy the devil prowls around like a roaring lion looking for someone to devour," is spot on. But while many Christians have taken steps to protect themselves, Satan is becoming more bold and crafty in his attacks on our children. If our own children are at risk, even with our vigilance, imagine the children without that protection. Like a

CHAPTER 2 – WHAT GOD KNOWS, SATAN EXPLOITS AND THE CHURCH HAS FORGOTTEN

lion picks out the young and defenseless, Satan targets the children of the world for indoctrination into his worldview because he knows, that if you raise up a child in the way that he should NOT go, even when he is old he will not depart from it.

What the Church has forgotten

"After that whole generation had been gathered to their ancestors, another generation grew up who knew neither the LORD nor what he had done for Israel." Judges 2:10

While the church has not always been in the dark regarding the urgent nature of teaching our children with excellence and reaching out to the children of the world, a strong case can be made that we have forgotten these God-given principles somewhere along the way.

> *Every year the world population is adding enough children to double the population of Russia and 70% are being born into non-Christian homes.*
>
> *Children make up 1/3 of the world population and roughly 27% of the church and yet, on*

> *average, only an <u>estimated</u> 3% [3] of ministry budgets are directed at reaching and teaching them.*

For years in missions we have focused on the so-called 10/40 window, a term coined by mission's strategist Luis Bush for the regions of the eastern hemisphere (between 10 and 40 degrees of the equator) with the greatest poverty and least access to the Gospel. At the turn of this century, reinforced by the publishing of George Barna's landmark work regarding ministry to children, "Transforming Children into Spiritual Champions," Mr. Bush introduced a new "window" into the Christian missionary lexicon. The "4/14 window," so named for the age window where most people meet Jesus and are transformed by his gospel. It is the age window where our worldview and personal character are formed. Just like the 10/40 window before it, the 4/14 window is meant to be a catalyst and rallying cry for focusing the time, talent and treasure of the church in a specific direction. More than a decade later the question is; is it working?

What are we doing? What should we do? What will be the churches' impact on the next generation? How do our

---

[3] 3% number is an estimation taken from an unpublished study conducted by a large, reputable missionary organization, using data from both inside and outside the United States.

investments stack up against our rhetoric? Are we aiming our time and treasure towards children in the church, in the family, and through local and international missions?

By and large the outlook is not good. We are on the ropes and in many cases not even facing in the right direction. I don't want to get into theories as to why this state of affairs exists because frankly it doesn't matter why. It only matters that we as the church recognize the error and make appropriate course corrections now. **Every moment that passes more and more children cross the fourteen-year threshold and, when they do, our job gets exceedingly more difficult.**

Imbalances within the Church

The child-care church

Many well-meaning church leaders will say, "Wait just a minute. The responsibility for the spiritual formation of children lies with the parents." But this is only a partially true statement. The commands to "teach your children" in the old and new testaments, while directed first at the parents, were also communal responsibilities and have been interpreted as such through all of Jewish history. It is a cop-out of enormous proportions when the church provides, "child-care," while parents worship and are taught, with the excuse being that meaningful Christian education should happen in the home. It should be happening in the home, yes, but also on the way and when they sit down and when they rise up, essentially everywhere, not least of all where the church gathers. We must also remember the child of the absent or unbelieving parent. The community of faith has a critical role.

It is time that the church woke up and reordered her priorities. The church must invest heavily in working with parents, encouraging and equipping them to disciple their "blessings from the Lord." Church leadership must spur on fathers to take the lead in the spiritual formation of their children. I, for one, will never abdicate my GOD given role of spiritual leader in my household. At the same time the church has a significant supporting role to play in raising up the next generation in the fear and admonition of the Lord, teaching the children what it means to be the church of Jesus Christ.

The "Go it alone" Parent

This phenomenon is not only the fault of the church. Perhaps you know a parent who doesn't see any role for the Church in the spiritual development of their child either. Believe it or not I had a parent say to me, regarding Sunday school, "All I'm looking for from the church is child-care while my wife and I worship. We handle all of their spiritual education." To this go it alone parent I would say, "Let me tell you a story." A pastor, friend, and excellent teacher, once relayed to me a story about one of his children. He had been teaching a particular theological truth to his child for years, seemingly to no avail, when one day the child returned home

CHAPTER 2 – WHAT GOD KNOWS, SATAN EXPLOITS AND THE CHURCH HAS FORGOTTEN

from church very excited to relay the "new" thing they had learned about GOD from Mr. So and So, their Sunday School teacher. My friend was shocked to find out it was the same thing he had been trying to teach his child all these years. For some reason GOD chose to use another teacher to drive this particular truth to the child's heart. The moral of this story is that GOD will bring many people along to build into the life of your children. You, as the parent and gatekeeper, should welcome and even seek out these inputs from your brothers and sisters in Christ. Don't isolate yourself in this most important and difficult battle when you have fellow soldiers ready and willing to support you.

The "I'm not qualified" parent

The other side of that coin, and the last of the imbalances in the church as it relates to children, is the parent who thinks that the spiritual formation of their children is something best left to the "professionals," the pastors and teachers of their church. When you combine this attitude with the "child care church" you have a recipe for disaster. Did you teach your child to walk, eat, speak, and dress him or herself or did you hire help for that? Did you teach your child the importance of a good diet, hygiene, doing homework, or keeping a clean room or did you hire a "pro" for these things? I could go on but the answer for these questions should be obvious. Then why on earth would you neglect the most important lessons they have to learn and leave those to someone who at best will spend about 40 hours a year with your child? Understand this, there is no one person more critical to the spiritual formation of your child than you. If you don't feel qualified then get qualified, but don't wait to begin to talk about the things of God with your children as you sit at home, as you walk along the way, when you lie down and when you rise up. Patrick Henry, one of the Founding Fathers of the United States, is quoted as saying this,

"I have now disposed of all my property to my family; there is one thing more I wish I could give them, and that is the Christian Religion. If they had that, and I had not given them one shilling, they would be rich; and if they had not that, and I had given them all the world, they would be poor."

Parents, and principally fathers, are the God-given spiritual leaders of their families. This means that every God fearing parent should be earnestly seeking to be committed to, equipped for and engaged in teaching their children in the way they should go.

"Both-And"

So which is it? Is it the parents' job or the church? The answer is, both and. Consider this question. Can you really have too many godly people pouring into the life of a child? We are all in this together. You, the parent, are commanded to teach, instruct, and model Christ to your children and this will look different in every family. That is a beautiful thing. The

CHAPTER 2 – WHAT GOD KNOWS, SATAN EXPLOITS AND THE CHURCH HAS FORGOTTEN

command is clear, but GOD allows for the very different gifting of each of us. He also has built His Church so that all parts of the body work together and have the benefit of the others. Reggie Joyner, in his book, "Parenting beyond your capacity," summed it up perfectly,

"When you combine the light from a faith community…with the heart of a caring family, you exponentially expand your potential to make a difference in the life of a child. These two influences will make a greater impact than either influence alone."

Sadly today, for much of the Christian world we are instead taking the "neither nor" approach. Consider just two of George Barna's findings regarding the grades the church and parents are getting in their task of helping children grow spiritually.

> *72% of parents say they're doing well in providing spiritual experience and instructions to their children, yet only 10% of church households spend **any** time at all during a typical week reading the Bible or praying together."*

> *"Most churches have very simple but ultimately debilitating descriptions of success: growing numbers of student's enrolled, consistent attendance, completion of the curriculum in the allotted time, parental satisfaction, and minimal discipline problems."*

Foreign language immersion, math tutors, sport specific training, piano lessons, and science camp. Does that sound like the line up for a sophomore in college? It's actually a small sampling of the academic and sporting pursuits common amongst elementary school age children in Northern Virginia, where I have lived with my wife and our three children. Friends, we are willing to spend untold thousands of dollars to give our children the very best in secular education. We hire experts because we want our children to have every opportunity for success. It is widely accepted that children have an amazing capability to learn at a very early age and the academic choices we make for our children bear this out. Why is it then that so many Christian parents are satisfied if their children can do little more than recite some basic facts about Noah and the flood, the birth of Jesus Christ, or the account of Daniel in the Lion's Den, but can tell us nothing of what we learn about our GOD or our relationship to Him through these accounts? Why are more parents not alarmed that many of our children can't explain, in simple terms, the gospel of salvation beyond repeating back the lingo they've grown up hearing. Ask a child what they mean by "having Jesus in your heart" and you may be shocked by their response or lack thereof.

We've been better

This is not what the church of Christ throughout history has been about.

CHAPTER 2 – WHAT GOD KNOWS, SATAN EXPLOITS AND THE CHURCH HAS FORGOTTEN

The West Minster Shorter Catechism was completed in 1647 with one of its chief uses being the education of children. This is no lightweight document. With such questions as "What do the scriptures principally teach?" and "What offices does Christ execute as redeemer?" I wonder how many adults in the church would be completely stumped. If only we as the Church would return to that standard for excellence. What a difference it would make in the lives of our children and in our congregations. Wouldn't it strike fear into the heart of our old adversary to see that the Church of Jesus had not abandoned the battle for the hearts of the children? That our children were fully armed with GOD's spiritual armor? I can almost feel the darkness tremble just at the thought.

So what is it exactly that the church has forgotten and needs to remember? I would submit the following statement for your consideration;

"It was he who gave...some to be pastors and teachers, to prepare GOD's people (not just the adults but all God's people) for works of service, so that the body of Christ may be built up" Ephesians 4:11-12.

All people, in all stages of life, are loved by GOD unconditionally. It is GOD's will, as is clearly and emphatically stated in scripture, that children be taught the deeper things of GOD by GOD's people, primarily but not exclusively, the parents. From this we can draw some basic truths.

- *People, in all stages of life, are of equal value to GOD*
- *Children who have trusted in Christ are NOT only the church of the future; they are the church of the present*
- *Children of the church need to be recognized as people of faith*
- *Children need to both contribute and receive as members of GOD's family*
- *Children must be invited to participate as the church in fellowship, worship, prayer, learning of the Word and service.*
- *Children need to be changed by the love of Christ and share the Gospel in their context.*
- *Christian nurture and growth are for all and are the responsibility of all.*
- *Parents must be equipped within the church to fulfill their role as primary spiritual leaders of their children.*
- *Children respond in much greater percentages to the gospel than their adult counterparts and therefore should command at least as much attention in our missionary efforts.*
- *Our investments in time, talent and treasure should reflect our commitment to these truths. "For where your treasure is, there your heart will be also." Luke 12:34*
- *Our success can only be measured by the spiritual growth of the children in our sphere of influence*

CHAPTER 2 – WHAT GOD KNOWS, SATAN EXPLOITS AND THE CHURCH HAS FORGOTTEN

Failure is not an option

I recently visited the Smithsonian Institutes Air and Space Museum near Dulles Airport in Virginia. While browsing through the gift shop I got a kick out of an interesting shirt being sold. It had the following phrase emblazoned across the front, "Failure is NOT an option." Next to that was written, "Apollo XIII Lunar Mission." A truer thing has never been said. If they had failed it would have meant an awful death for the astronauts onboard and a great national tragedy.

That shirt got me thinking. What if we fail? What if the "best we can" isn't good enough? What if we don't invest appropriately in teaching our children and reaching the children around us with the gospel? The good news is we don't have to theorize or guess about the repercussions of failure because it has happened before. Joshua, the great and faithful military leader of GOD's people Israel, who led them into the Promised Land and defeated their enemies, failed in one very critical area as a leader. The tragedy unfolds in the book of Judges.

"After that whole generation had been gathered to their
ancestors, another generation grew up who knew neither the
LORD nor what he had done for Israel. Then the Israelites did
evil in the eyes of the LORD and served the Baals. They
forsook the LORD, the GOD of their ancestors, who had

brought them out of Egypt. They followed and worshiped various gods of the peoples around them. They aroused the LORD's anger" Judges 2:10 -12

The consequences of failing to adequately teach the children is that they will "not know the Lord" and because of that lack of knowledge they will fall into the hands of this world system, turning their backs on the living GOD. The outcome for their families and communities is predictable. All of the time, talent and treasure we have invested in so many other important ministries directed toward adult people will be lost as the last member of that generation joins their ancestors. Is that the spiritual legacy we want to leave? **Who will disciple the children, the people of GOD or the world?**

Failure is not an option. The stakes are far too high.

Chapter 3 - Defenses Down

"But my eyes are toward you, O GOD, my Lord; in you I seek refuge; leave me not defenseless!" Psalm 141:8

CHAPTER 3 – DEFENSES DOWN

So now we should understand the truths that GOD commands us to teach children, and that He has hardwired them to respond to and embrace this teaching when done well and in the context of loving relationships. We have stated that Satan also recognizes this and thus targets the children in an attempt to steal away a generation. We have also made the case that the Church must refocus its time, talent and treasure in response if we are to raise a generation that knows and respects the Lord.

"Only an estimated 3% of church budgets are dedicated to reaching and teaching children"

We know much more about ourselves and the way GOD has wired us as human beings. However, if we are to be victorious, we must also understand a bit more about the tactics of our adversary.

Why has Satan been so successful at getting to the children? What weakness of ours is he exploiting, what areas in our defenses have been compromised?

As the Chinese General, Sun Tzu wrote in his classic, "The Art of War," "So it is said that if you know your enemies and know yourself, you can win a hundred battles without a single loss."

Satan is "shaping" the battlefield

Whether we are discussing a street fight, modern military tactics, ancient city defenses or home protection, certain principles apply.

Definition: Shaping the Battlefield: Eliminate the enemy's capability to fight in a coherent manner before committing forces. Set the conditions for success in decisive operations.

On March 19th, 2003 the second Persian Gulf War began when American Stealth bombers and Tomahawk missiles struck "leadership targets" deep within Iraq, opening the door for a massive and rapid infantry assault that would quickly overwhelm Saddam Hussein's forces. Interestingly, heavy bombing has preceded most great invasions since the dawn of the cannon. In the military jargon, artillery bombardment "shapes" the battlefield giving infantry the greatest chance for decisive victory. It just makes sense that any well-conducted military assault would begin with taking out, demoralizing or otherwise incapacitating the targets defenses and leaders. Removing leadership, jamming radar systems, eliminating air defense systems, destroying command and control structures and disrupting supply lines are all keys to causing confusion and overthrowing a kingdom. Even before the age of modern warfare, cannon

CHAPTER 3 – DEFENSES DOWN

bombardment broke down castle walls, allowing foot soldiers to spill through the gaps in order to inflict untold damage on those seeking protection within. When leadership is gone, the chain of command is broken and the defensive walls have been breached, it's every man for his self. Chaos ensues and those left go into survival mode. In physical war this tactic is obvious because of the "shock and awe" nature of modern weaponry and speed with which things happen.

Spiritual war is not so different. Our enemy's use of this same tactic, however, can be so subtle, to those not paying attention, that by the time we realize an attack is under way, we have already been overrun. As mentioned earlier, Satan's objective is clearly laid out by Jesus in John chapter 10, verse 10 where he says, "The thief (Satan) comes only to steal and kill and destroy." If your aim were essentially to cause chaos and confusion, promoting everything that is contrary to GOD's Kingdom, the first strategic initiative would be to <u>remove or render useless that Kingdom's defenses</u>. As a predator Satan seeks out the weak, the young, those separated from the herd and defenseless. The children of the world are part of this group.

So, what or who constitutes the defense system GOD has put in place for children? Let's look to scripture. There we see that Biblical defense, provision, rescue, and strength giving is provided by Abba, Father. As children of GOD we pray, "Our **Father**, who is in heaven…" and trust in Him to protect, provide for, teach and guide us. David calls the Father "my Rock", "my strong tower", "my salvation" and speaks of being hidden in the "shadow of His wings." Jesus proclaims, "In the same way your **Father** in heaven is not willing that any of these little ones should perish." (Matthew 18:14)

GOD in his wisdom created the family and placed at its head an earthly father whose role as defender, provider, teacher and friend were meant to reflect those same qualities found in our heavenly Father.

*"For I too was a son to my **father**, still tender, and cherished by my mother. Then he taught me, and he said to me, "Take hold of my words with all your heart; keep my commands, and you will live. (Proverbs 4:3-4, emphasis added)*

Does GOD's design work? Many of you who suffered under disengaged or abusive fathers would say no. But that kind of father was not GOD's design at all. The fact is that when a child lives in the presence of a godly father, one who is **committed** to modeling a Christ centered life, one who is being **equipped** by God's Word, one who is actively **engaged** in teaching the truth within the context of a loving and safe relationship, he or she is at nearly zero risk for things like drug or alcohol use, violence, and suicide. The power of a committed, equipped and lovingly engaged Father, living out his faith before his children, is not to be underestimated.

So then, if you are planning an attack with the goal of creating chaos...

(The thief comes only to steal and kill and destroy;(John 10:10a))

CHAPTER 3 – DEFENSES DOWN

...then you would surely want to eliminate or otherwise neutralize this very powerful defensive mechanism we call the godly father. Removing him from families, from communities and from the church would be a critical first phase in any well-planned attack on those institutions and the children in general.

To put us in the right frame of mind I would like to introduce you to three young people who became casualties of these attacks.

Eduardo

Their seemingly orderly life began to come apart the night their little two-room house caught fire. The little boy, one of five siblings, couldn't begin to fathom the significance of this moment and the cascade of events that would flow from it, as he sat quietly across the street watching his family's life go up in smoke. His father, who until then had been a responsible, hard-working man, was so shaken by the tragedy that he turned to the bottle. His mother, a Christian woman, became increasingly bitter with his drinking and the violence and infidelity that came along with it. The family moved to a tough neighborhood in a new town looking for work and a new start. This further severed ties with relatives and friends leading the young family to become isolated.

As the environment at home became increasingly tense the boy escaped to the streets during the day, returning home just to sleep and eat. As time went on, school became ever more difficult for him. He couldn't sit still, and chafed at the discipline in the classroom. Not even the one Christian physical education teacher who took an interest and tried to reach out to him was able to keep the troubled youngster engaged. One school after another expelled him for indiscipline until even his classmates signed a petition to have him removed. Eduardo, or Du as he came to be called, turned to the streets and there found acceptance. In the street he found friends who shared his dislike and distrust of authority, friends who, like him, had no father to show them what it meant to be a man. They experimented with alcohol and then drugs and liked the feeling of freedom that it gave them. They discovered that as a group they could be quite intimidating, forcing weaker children and then teens and eventually adults to give up their money. When this didn't satisfy, they turned to burglaries, robbing houses across town and then retreating to the safety of their neighborhood.

They made quite a name for themselves and the older boys in the neighborhood eventually took notice and recruited them for small time trafficking of marijuana and crack cocaine. Du's distraught and overwhelmed mother prayed for him but seemed unable to overcome her own trials in order to get through to her son. A head on collision with the law seemed inevitable.

On one particular evening he and some friends travelled across town to burglarize a house they believed would be empty. As they approached the outer wall he

CHAPTER 3 – DEFENSES DOWN

sensed something wrong in the pit of his stomach and told his boys to back off. They wouldn't rob this house today. He wouldn't discover the source of this ill feeling until more than two years later. The boys were peddling across town lamenting their failed mission when they came upon an older gentleman heading home after a day's work. The decision to shake him down was made in an instant. At least they wouldn't go home empty handed. Eduardo and his crew didn't get much from their assault but it was better than nothing and as they turned into their neighborhood there came the safe feeling that goes with being on your home turf.

This made the squad cars that seemed to materialize out of nowhere all the more surprising. Bicycles crashed to the ground. The teens tried to run but there was just nowhere to go. As the officers threw them to the ground and began to beat and curse at them, Eduardo thought, "I'm going to die here and no one is coming to help me." At sixteen years of age he was sent first to an adult penitentiary where he would await his trial. Du was kept in a cell separate from the more hardened adult prisoners. Fifteen minutes of sunlight per day for thirty days. It seemed like it would never end. His trial came and with several outstanding warrants he was given the maximum for a juvenile offender. He would serve out his time in the infamous FEBEM juvenile prison system of Brazil, never hearing from a single "friend," his only visitor being his mother. But then he got a letter that would change everything…

Lucas

He never even knew that something was wrong. There had never been a father in their home so he didn't know to miss one. When the little ones were left alone to fend for themselves while mom travelled to another city, supposedly looking for work, it wasn't long before a concerned neighbor called social services to report that there were young children living alone without adult care.

Lucas would spend the next five years in a shelter for abandoned children about forty-five minutes from his hometown. Once he got used to the physical abuse from older children and some of the monitors he got along well there. There were outings and school and horses. The only family he had ever known, a sister and brother, was there with him. They looked out for each other and the time passed.

One-day mom showed up. She had gotten married and the couple had come to claim the children. This new man would adopt Lucas and give him his last name. Things were looking up. Sadly, cirrhosis from many years of alcohol abuse would soon take the new man away and mom would let the children fall into neglect once again.

Lucas had had enough. Home had become a place not of safety but of violence and hunger. At ten years of age he showed up on the doorstep of an elderly woman he knew through his deceased stepfather and she took him in. Living in one of the toughest neighborhoods in town, no father, no one to show him what it means to be a man, it wasn't long

CHAPTER 3 – DEFENSES DOWN

before he found some older boys who offered acceptance into their world of drugs, violence and petty crime. Lucas' indiscipline and poor attendance at school eventually caught the attention of city officials and he was selected to attend a new reform school, once again shipped off because he was too much "trouble." At the new school, a gathering of the worst of the worst from the city's overburdened school system, their first "field trip" would change his life forever…

Mariana

Normal is in the eye of the beholder. For Mariana, who has grown up in a neighborhood notorious for drug trafficking and violence; police raids, gang shootings, and prostitution are part of the "normal" landscape. Living in a two-room structure with her mother, two adult sisters and nine other children, Mariana has been a caregiver from a very young age. There were never adult men in the home for very long. Her own father has been in prison much of her life, along with an older brother. Another brother began working for the local drug boss when he was just twelve years old. He started as a courier and moved his way up to enforcer before he was picked up in a police raid at the age of 14 and sent to a juvenile detention center.

Mariana helped make money for the family by selling pastries and occasionally carrying an unmarked package from here to there for the local traffickers. No questions asked. In a neighborhood where 70% of the population is involved in the drug trade to some extent, this was all "normal." Mariana struggled in school with her grades and with discipline. She was tough and angry. She had to be to get along in her world. Mariana's life was leading down the same path as her older sisters who had become single mothers in their teens. She had never been someone's "princess." A loving father, a godly friend, or a safe place to just be a child were all foreign concepts until the day a concerned city health worker took an interest and sought out help…

Sorry to have to leave you hanging, but before I tell you the rest of these stories we need to fortify our understanding of the damage our adversary has been able to inflict.

The Strong Man

Jesus, when explaining how it was he could expel demons, said,

> *"How can anyone enter a strong man's house and carry off his possessions unless he first ties up the strong man? Then he can plunder his house." (Matthew 12:29)*

In the same way, how can Satan enter the house of a strong man and steal the hearts of his children if he doesn't first tie up that strong man? The answer is obvious, He can't. The father is Satan's target number one in his attack on the family, civil society and the Church. Knowing that the father is the main line of defense, we must now have an honest

CHAPTER 3 – DEFENSES DOWN

assessment of the condition of those defenses. In much the same way as the biblical leader Nehemiah set out to inspect the walls of Jerusalem, we need to mount up together and ride out to inspect the condition of GOD's ordained defensive structures.

"By night I went out through the Valley Gate toward the Jackal Well and the Dung Gate, examining the walls of Jerusalem" Nehemiah 2:13a

Holes in the Wall

Sadly, across all levels of society, but especially among the poor, Satan has had great success in eliminating the strong man. He has used a wide variety of tools including addiction, pornography, popular culture, liberalized divorce laws, the modern feminist movement and government welfare programs that seek to replace the father and encourage out-of-wedlock births. In this way he has effectively removed the strong man from many families, communities and even the church. According to the US census bureau, some 24 million children live in fatherless homes. Those 24 million American children are without their major protector, provider, teacher and friend. Today 40% of all children in the United States are born to single mothers. Outside the US the picture isn't any better. In Brazil, for example, 700,000 children are born each year without a father figure. Roughly 30% of the entire population of Brazil doesn't shop for a gift on Father's Day because they don't know the man. These children are incredibly vulnerable. Just consider for a moment the pounding they are taking -

> **Incarceration Rates.** *"Young men who grow up in homes without fathers are twice as likely to end up in jail as those who come from traditional two-parent families...those boys whose fathers were absent from the household had double the odds of being incarcerated -- even when other factors such as race, income, parent education and urban residence were held constant." (Cynthia Harper of the University of Pennsylvania and Sara S. McLanahan of Princeton University cited in "Father Absence and Youth Incarceration." Journal of Research on Adolescence 14 (September 2004): 369-397.)That is not of course including the millions of children with unengaged, abusive or negligent fathers that live at home.*
>
> **Suicide.** *63% of youth suicides are from fatherless homes (U.S. Department of Health and Human Services, Bureau of the Census)*
>
> **Behavioral Disorders.** *85% of all children that exhibit behavioral disorders come from fatherless homes (United States Center for Disease Control)*
>
> **High School Dropouts**. *71% of all high school dropouts come from fatherless homes (National Principals Association Report on the State of High Schools.)*

CHAPTER 3 – DEFENSES DOWN

Educational Attainment. *Kids living in single-parent homes or in step-families report lower educational expectations on the part of their parents, less parental monitoring of school work, and less overall social supervision than children from intact families. (N.M. Astore and S. McLanahan, American Sociological Review, No. 56 (1991)*

Juvenile Detention Rates. *70% of juveniles in state-operated institutions come from fatherless homes (U.S. Dept. of Justice, Special Report, Sept 1988)*

Confused Identities. *Boys who grow up in father-absent homes are more likely than those in father-present homes to have trouble establishing appropriate sex roles and gender identity.(P.L. Adams, J.R. Milner, and N.A. Schrepf, Fatherless Children, New York, Wiley Press, 1984).*

Aggression. *In a longitudinal study of 1,197 fourth-grade students, researchers observed "greater levels of aggression in boys from mother-only households than from boys in mother-father households." (N. Vaden-Kierman, N. Ialongo, J. Pearson, and S. Kellam, "Household Family Structure and Children's Aggressive Behavior: A Longitudinal Study of Urban Elementary School*

Children," Journal of Abnormal Child Psychology 23, no. 5 (1995).

Achievement. *Children from low-income, two-parent families outperform students from high-income, single-parent homes. Almost twice as many high achievers come from two-parent homes as one-parent homes. (One-Parent Families and Their Children, Charles F. Kettering Foundation, 1990).*

Delinquency. *Only 13 percent of juvenile delinquents come from families in which the biological mother and father are married to each other. By contract, 33 percent have parents who are either divorced or separated and 44 percent have parents who were never married. (Wisconsin Dept. of Health and Social Services, April 1994).*

Criminal Activity. *The likelihood that a young male will engage in criminal activity doubles if he is raised without a father and triples if he lives in a neighborhood with a high concentration of single-parent families. Source: A. Anne Hill, June O'Neill, Underclass Behaviors in the United States, CUNY, Baruch College. 1993*

Devastation

Research and years of experience have shown without a doubt that fatherlessness leads to material poverty, poor physical and mental health, crime, violence, drug and alcohol addiction, a general breakdown in social connectedness within a community, higher infant mortality rates, promiscuity and an increase in out-of-wedlock births. If these are not the kinds of things that come to mind when we read, "The thief comes only to steal and kill and destroy;" then I don't know what are. With the "strong man" out of the picture, the deck is stacked against the children. We only need to think back to my friends, Eduardo, Lucas, and Mariana, to see the likely outcome for these young people. All were, for different reasons, without a father to protect, to provide, to teach and to love. Without this figure they were left to seek out models elsewhere.

The realization that Satan has been so successful in removing the God-given defenders of the family, and of civil society, should shock and alarm us. The damage he has been able to inflict as a result should break our hearts as they break the heart of our heavenly Father.

Strong man Technical Knock-out

An even scarier realization is that fatherlessness is not limited to the complete absence of dad. The key to protecting our children from Satan's schemes, as we stated earlier, is the presence of a "godly" and "engaged" father, in loving relationship with his children. This distinction cannot be over-emphasized. **Just any old dad simply won't do and even a good father can be taken out of the fight.** Researchers at

Columbia University found that children living in a two-parent household with a poor relationship with their father are 68% more likely to smoke, drink, or use drugs compared to all teens in two-parent households.[4] So we see that Satan still packs a punch even if he can only temporarily or partially incapacitate the "strong man" by getting him to take his eye off the ball.

Grandpa Meyers

Early one morning in my sixth grade year my mother answered the phone just as we were heading out the door for school. It was my grandmother who lived nearby, calling for help because she was having trouble waking Grandpa. My paternal grandfather, Frank H. Meyers, had died peacefully in his sleep. We were all hit hard by his unexpected passing. I cannot ever recall feeling such terrible loss or sadness before that time or since. But despite the initial shock of losing the patriarch of our family, what would unfold as the months and years passed, would dwarf it in terms of shear destructive force. My grandfather took very seriously the commands to "love justice, seek mercy and walk humbly with your GOD" as well as to "love your neighbor as yourself." He was one of 237 souls who had given his life to Jesus Christ one evening at

---

[4] *"Survey Links Teen Drug Use, Relationship With Father." Alcoholism & Drug Abuse Weekly 6 September 1999: 5.)*

CHAPTER 3 – DEFENSES DOWN

a Billy Graham crusade held in September of 1952 at the old Forbes Field in Pittsburgh, Pennsylvania and, for as long as I knew him, was a wonderful man of GOD, a rock in his church, always available to lend a hand to a neighbor in need. I never heard him utter a negative word about a soul. He was the glue that held our family together. What I absorbed from him was his belief that life was simple if we would just let GOD's Word be a "lamp to our feet and a light to our path." He exercised his moral authority in our family in a gentle but powerful way and we loved him for it.

It is never easy for a family to lose such a central figure so unexpectedly and my father never really recovered. The close relationship I had had with my dad in my early years, the moral teaching and good example he was for me were fond memories that seemed to begin to slowly erode away in my teen years as his own foundation was shaken. I love my dad very much and cherish my childhood memories. Just remembering these events and imagining his sadness and pain at the loss of his father brings tears to my eyes. It seemed like he began to lose his moral compass and bearings as a father and a husband. His crisis, which eventually led to the breakup of his marriage, could not have come at a worse time for his adolescent son. Even though I had asked Jesus to be my savior five years earlier, I was now at a critical time in my development when I needed more than ever a strong godly male role model to keep me from going off track. I was entering adolescence. The hormones were flowing. I was trying to define myself as a young man and at the same time questioning my own faith. This was a crossroads moment where I needed a father to talk openly to me about what it means to be a man of GOD, how to take ownership of my faith, how to think about and treat women, how to develop self-control and so many other lessons. My dad, in his sadness over the loss of his own father and what I perceived to be a moral and spiritual crisis, was effectively taken out of the game, leaving his own children vulnerable to our enemy's schemes.

I was left to find my role models in older "popular" kids, old NFL films and movies. I sought out other young men I could identify with. The model I found there was the "man" who had a girl on each arm, was in the middle of every fight, could drink into the wee hours and still win the big game the next morning. Within a year of my grandfather's death I was experimenting with alcohol, sneaking out of the house in the middle of the night, getting in to fights and "dating" one young lady after another. In my mind I was becoming a "man." I was twelve years old. I take full responsibility for my poor decisions during those years, but the fact remains that, by my father not taking the standard from grandpa Frank and carrying it for his wife and children, the thief who comes to steal, kill and destroy had succeeded in tying up the "strong man" in our family. It would be nine long years of wrestling with GOD and my own conscience before I would return to my heavenly Father and many more years after that before I would fully reconcile my relationship with my dad.

CHAPTER 3 – DEFENSES DOWN

If you are a dad, I ask you, have you let personal tragedy, work demands, selfishness, or any number of other distractions cause you to drop your guard? Have you left your wife and children unprotected? Men, we cannot let our guard down even for an instant. Our enemy the devil is just waiting to land a sucker punch.

"Be alert and of sober mind. Your enemy the devil prowls around like a roaring lion looking for someone to devour." 1 Peter 5:8

We are losing ground in...

The family

Carol is the oldest of three siblings. She has two younger brothers; half-brothers to be more precise. They all share one birth mother but different biological fathers. Carol's father is married and has another family across town. She doesn't ever see him but she is perhaps the lucky one. The father of her next youngest brother went to prison for drug trafficking and was drowned there in the toilet. Her brother now receives a small pension but he'd rather have his dad. The father of the youngest boy never made it to prison as he was executed at home for an outstanding drug debt. Carol carries a large portion of the responsibility for the care of the boys and has, ever since she was about 9 years old. Her mother holds jobs on and off and they live with their maternal grandmother and an Aunt. In this one case we see three common causes for the absent male in poor families;

promiscuity and general unwillingness to take responsibility for offspring, incarceration, and violence. In all three cases the results are the same. Children are raised in female led homes, older siblings are pressed into child rearing responsibilities, and the entire family sinks into a mode of survival where healthy connections to community institutions, like the church and schools, are weakened as the family's focus turns to meeting basic physical needs.

As recently as the 1960's, the vast majority of children still lived in dual parent homes. Contrast that with the current situation where 50% of all children will experience a single parent home for at least a portion of their childhood. This number is significantly higher in poor communities where incarceration and violence are added on top of the divorce and out-of-wedlock birth epidemics as causes of fatherlessness. Our organization, Open Arms Worldwide, works in communities in Brazil where 80-90% of the families are without an adult male in the home. These families are most often led by what I will call, "functional widows," women who are not technically widowed, but by virtue of abandonment are in fact functioning as such. Sadly, even when the family is blessed to have a present and employed father it is not always much better. The modern urban socio-economic structure, in which we live, different from the days of old, requires that the father work long hours some distance from home, leaving him less present in the daily life of his family and the community. He is fulfilling his role as provider but not the other three pillars of protector, teacher and friend. The bottom line is that across the world and

CHAPTER 3 – DEFENSES DOWN

across so called class lines, but more acutely in poor families, fathers are falling fast under a barrage of body blows from our enemy.

We are losing ground in…

The Community

What happens in a community where adult men, fathers, are absent? In poor or "high-risk" communities elevated rates of drug abuse and incarceration among the male population lead to a downward spiral of community disintegration. As adult men disappear from the community there is an increase in "street activity" where traditional community structures are replaced with informal ones such as street gangs and other criminal organizations. These groups further promote the drug culture leading to even more incarceration and violence, and the further fragmentation of families and community structures. This leads to a mostly misplaced distrust of police among children who watch their fathers and neighbors arrested. This in turn grows in to a general distrust of community authorities. Convicts are less "employable" upon release, further stimulating the economic sub-culture of drugs and prostitution. Rather than counting on the community to assist in rearing and disciplining children, parents that remain are forced into a protective stance. In her paper entitled, "Bearing the Burden: How Incarceration Weakens Inner-City Communities", Joan Moore,

LAST MAN STANDING

Ph.D. of the University of Wisconsin-Milwaukee writes about these special challenges.

> "There is a voluminous body of literature on the perils of child-rearing in communities with high levels of street activity. Parents in high-risk neighborhoods expend an enormous amount of effort sheltering and protecting their children (Williams & Kornblum, 1994). Constructive neighborhood networks become very important for effective parenting. In their absence, parents "must be super motivated, that is, exceptionally adept at working the system and unusually diligent in monitoring their offspring . . . avoiding the omnipresent dangers [rather] than cultivating scarce opportunities" (Furstenberg, 1993, p. 255). Effective parenting is quite different in such communities compared with low-risk neighborhoods."

In communities where fatherlessness is rampant, or in other words, where the command and control structure, the defensive systems, have been compromised, those left behind have to fend for themselves in an "every man for his self" struggle for survival. This is a cycle that, if not broken by some outside intervention, will continue and grow unchecked. A playground for Satan's plans to kill, steal and destroy.

We are losing ground in...

CHAPTER 3 – DEFENSES DOWN

The Church

Where should we find a bulwark against the plan of Satan to take down the "Strong man" defense system? Who is the "last man standing," that GOD put in place if not the Church of Jesus Christ? The Church and its men should be an impenetrable fortress, protecting their children from the enemy of their souls. Beyond that it should be a source of reinforcements for the families and communities who are losing their fathers. Certainly in the Church we should find men, followers of Christ, committed to fulfilling their role of provider, protector, teacher and friend.

So where are they? Again, some recent sociological research provides less than encouraging news for those children suffering on the front lines of fatherlessness. It is not my purpose here to theorize on the causes (that is one bull's-eye I do not wish to paint on my back), but the reality is stark as it regards men in the Church.

"Are males really less religious than females? Most of the studies made on the question seem to indicate that they are, and this appears to be true for all the Christian churches, denominations, and sects in western civilization." [5]*– James H. Fitcher,*

"women are twice as likely to attend a church service during any given week. Women are also 50 percent more likely than men to say

---

[5] James H. Fichter, "Why Aren't Males So Holy?" *Integrity* (May 1955): p. 3.

they are 'religious' and to state that they are 'absolutely committed' to the Christian faith." – George Barna,

"Church attendance in the United States is about 60 percent female and 40 percent male. The more liberal the denomination, the higher the percentage of females."[6]   – Leon J. Podles,

"Women, more often than not, take the lead role in the spiritual life of the family," "Women typically emerge as the primary -- or only -- spiritual mentor and role model for family members. And that puts a tremendous burden on wives and mothers." – George Barna[7]

The news out of Western Europe is much the same, and in Brazil the numbers are almost identical, with the ratio of Christian women to men at roughly 57/43% according to the IBGE – Instituto Brasileiro de Geografia e Estatístic in their 2000 census report.

While good people can disagree as to the cause of the masculinity deficit in the church, whether it is the feminization of sermons, worship and teaching in the church, liberal theology, a lack of vision driven churches or a generally feminized view of Christ and Christianity dating back to before the Reformation, there can be no disagreement

---

[6] *Leon J. Podles, "Missing Fathers of the Church"*

[7] George Barna,*Index of Leading Spiritual Indicators*(Dallas: Word Publishing, 1996),p.87.

CHAPTER 3 – DEFENSES DOWN

over the plain fact that many Christian churches in the world today are not producing "strong men," and those that are, by and large, are not sending them out into the world to stand in the gap for children who have been left defenseless by Satan's schemes.

"By night I went out through the Valley Gate toward the Jackal Well and the Dung Gate, examining the walls of Jerusalem, which had been broken down, and its gates, which had been destroyed by fire. Then I moved on toward the Fountain Gate and the King's Pool, but there was not enough room for my mount to get through; so I went up the valley by night, examining the wall. Finally, I turned back and reentered through the Valley Gate. The officials did not know where I had gone or what I was doing, because as yet I had said nothing to the Jews or the priests or nobles or officials or any others who would be doing the work.

Then I said to them, "You see the trouble we are in: Jerusalem lies in ruins, and its gates have been burned with fire. Come, let us rebuild the wall of Jerusalem, and we will no longer be in disgrace." I also told them about the gracious hand of my GOD on me and what the king had said to me.

They replied, "Let us start rebuilding." So they began this good work." Nehemiah 2:13-18

Our assessment is complete and the news is not good. It is downright discouraging to be exact. I echo Nehemiah when I ask, "Do you see the trouble we are in?"

You may be asking yourself now, "Why did I pick up this book? There is enough bad news in the world to wallow in and now this!" That could not be further from my intention here but I believe it is important to not understate the gravity of the situation, and to make clear the truth that the answer lies with us, the body of Jesus Christ, the Church.

The body of Christ is the "last man standing"

While leading a team from a church in Brazil on a mission to work with children in a neighborhood that had grown up around the city trash dump, one of our team members and a dear friend, upon seeing the poverty, unsanitary conditions and widespread fatherlessness, commented, "Where is our government!? Why is this allowed to go on?" My answer to him, and others that might think that the government, or any other institution, holds the key, is this, "The root of the problems of fatherlessness, poverty and crime are not only, or even primarily, physical, educational or financial, but spiritual, and the church of Jesus **alone** is capable of answering all of these needs."

Civil Servants of the Kingdom

The responsibility for addressing these needs does indeed belong to the government, but not the earthly one my friend had in mind. The job belongs to the civil servants of GOD's Kingdom and that means you and me. If you are a man

CHAPTER 3 – DEFENSES DOWN

reading this you might be thinking, "Here we go, another thing I am responsible for." But let me assure you, this is not another hammer to pound men over the head with. We have enough of those today. These are GOD sized problems that no one of us alone, man or woman, can completely remedy. The answers lie with the whole family of GOD empowered by the grace of God through Christ. Nehemiah did not call only on the men to stand in the gap and rebuild the walls, but rather for the men to lead their families in this great endeavor.

> "Therefore I stationed some of the people behind the lowest points of the wall at the exposed places, posting them by **_families_**, with their swords, spears and bows." Nehemiah 4:13 (emphasis added)

We have done it before. Just consider this excerpt from an article written by Timothy Larsen for the web site Christianhistory.net about the early Sunday school movement.

> "By the mid-19th century, Sunday school attendance was a near universal aspect of childhood. Even parents who did not regularly attend church themselves generally insisted that their children go to Sunday school. Working-class families were grateful for this opportunity to receive an education. They also looked forward to annual highlights such as prize days, parades, and picnics, which came to mark the calendars of their lives as much as more traditional seasonal holidays.

LAST MAN STANDING

Religious education was, of course, always also a core component. The Bible was the textbook used for learning to read. Likewise, many children learned to write by copying out passages from the Scriptures. A basic catechism was also taught, as were spiritual practices such as prayer and hymn singing. Inculcating Christian morality and virtues was another goal of the movement. Sunday school pupils often graduated to become Sunday school teachers, thereby gaining an experience of leadership not to be found elsewhere in their lives."

Far from gloom and doom, my hearts desire is to hear the Church of Jesus Christ say with gusto, *"Let us start rebuilding,"* and begin the good work of reestablishing our defenses and going on the offensive for the hearts of children in GOD's Kingdom.

"I looked for someone among them who would build up the wall and stand before me in the gap on behalf of the land..." Ezekiel 22:30a

Chapter 4 - God is in your corner so come out swinging!

CHAPTER 4 – GOD IS IN YOUR CORNER SO COME OUT SWINGING!

"You are coming to fight against me with a sword, a spear and a javelin. But I'm coming against you in the name of the Lord who rules over all. He is the God of the armies of Israel. He's the one you have dared to fight against.

1 Samuel 17:45

Let's come up and take a breath for a moment. Are you feeling a little overwhelmed? Take heart, I have been where you are. It's a lot to take in. We have learned of **the special place children hold in the heart of GOD and how He has commanded his people to take seriously the task of teaching them.** We have explored the very unique way we as GOD's creation are "wired" and why that "wiring" makes it critical as parents and the church to reach all children early with quality, relational discipleship. We have exposed Satan's strategy for leaving the children in your family, church, neighborhood and around the world vulnerable to his plans by tying up the "strong man."

So now is the big moment when we should be asking ourselves, "What do I do with this information?" Will I reorder my priorities so that I am fully engaged in discipling my children? Will I engage my church leadership to encourage them to make our biblical instruction and treatment of children more robust and effective? Will I get more involved in encouraging other men in the church to follow me in this? I pray that the answer to all of these questions is a resounding "Yes!" But there is more. There is a place beyond our church walls where the fight is even more intense, a bare knuckle place where the potential for heartbreak and frustration are only off-set by the enormous blessings to be enjoyed. It is a place of a most Christ-like sacrifice where the object of your gift is powerless to give anything in return.

Prepare your Heart

We have analyzed the dire situation the children are in and developed intelligence regarding our enemy and the damage he has been able to inflict, now what? If you are committed to the fight, you must equip yourself for the confrontation, because, make no mistake; Satan will not give up this ground easily. Thankfully, in addition to the Bible, there are some excellent resources available to us. The following books have influenced my journey profoundly and I trust that they will prepare your heart as well.

For the man who is seeking to become what GOD designed him to be, I recommend, "Tender Warrior" by Stu Weber as a great place to start. For parents and church leaders wishing to do better at raising a generation that knows the Lord, I would suggest, "Transforming Children into Spiritual Champions" by George Barna, "Sacred Parenting" by Gary Thomas, "Shepherding a child's heart" by Tedd Tripp, "Bringing up boys" and "Bringing up Girls" by Dr. James

CHAPTER 4 – GOD IS IN YOUR CORNER SO COME OUT SWINGING!

Dobson and "Parenting Beyond your Capacity" by Reggie Joiner and Carey Nieuwhof. These are just a few of the many amazing books, written by gifted, godly men who have looked deeply into scripture regarding these subjects. I have read them each at least once and recommend them all highly to those of you who are now awakening to some of the shocking information we've just reviewed together.

Moving Beyond

From here on out we are moving into uncharted territory. As I have said before, it isn't enough to simply care for, physically and spiritually, our children and the children in our church family. These roles of course, are biblical, foundational and well established throughout Christian literature and the Church in greater or lesser degrees since the resurrection of Christ. But is that where our responsibility ends? I believe GOD's answer is no.

The fact is that the fatherless outside the church far outnumber our own children and the majority of the children born in the world today are born into non-Christian homes.

Everything we have learned about children in our families and the church leads us inevitably to the children in our community and the world. Circling the wagons to make a stand leaves the majority of the world's future generations outside the circle. Are you willing to give them up without a fight? Is that how we operate, as the Church of Jesus, the "last man standing?" I hope the answer is no because if you think Satan puts up a fight when we start spiritually leading our own children, you haven't seen anything. The moment we move beyond the boundaries of the church family we enter into hostile territory indeed. But that is exactly where I believe God is calling us. If not us, then who?

READ ON AT YOUR OWN RISK

CHAPTER 4 – GOD IS IN YOUR CORNER SO COME OUT SWINGING!

*"**Be imitators of GOD**, therefore, as dearly loved children"*

Ephesians 5:1 (emphasis added)

The Sincerest Form of Flattery

I am a simple man, not a great theologian, and I tend to read and understand scripture in a straightforward way. The Bible makes plain that, when we are reborn in Christ, we are called to be "imitators of GOD," that is, imitators of his communicable character attributes, those attributes GOD "shares" with his adopted children. We can know the character of our GOD because it is clearly revealed in scripture. God is loving, patient, kind, good, joyful, faithful, forgiving, generous, courageous, and holy just to name a few. These are traits we should strive to imitate.

As "dearly loved children" we are also to imitate the things the Father does. Jesus says in John 5:19, "Very truly I tell you, the Son can do nothing by himself; he can do only what he sees his Father doing, because whatever the Father does the Son also does." Does this carry over to the adopted sons (believers) as well? Jesus implies that it does when he goes on to say in John 14:12, "I tell you the truth, anyone who has faith in me will do what I have been doing. He will do even greater things than these, because I am going to the Father."

A GOD size assignment

Be "imitators" of GOD. Now, if you are like me, that is an amazing and yet frightening command. To be honest, at first glance it sounds like yet another impossibly high bar to jump and frankly a little burdensome. For me it ranks right up there with, "Be holy as I am holy," in terms of potentially discouraging expectations. But at closer examination, it really is the promise of living in the presence and power of our Father, enjoying his company and learning while working at his side.

Notice what Jesus did not say. He did not say, "anyone who has faith in me will **be required to** do what I have been doing. Or **be required** to do even greater things than these." Instead, Jesus uses an affirmative statement, saying that anyone who has faith in me "will" do what I have been doing and "will" do even greater things. The idea here is that, as adopted children of GOD, walking in the Spirit, we will **want** to be imitators of our Father, not forced, and that we are empowered by Christ himself, to do these things. That should be exciting and encouraging news. What dearly loved child doesn't want to imitate dad?

CHAPTER 4 – GOD IS IN YOUR CORNER SO COME OUT SWINGING!

Dad is at your side

Let's look even more closely at part of that statement. Jesus said, "Whatever the Father does the Son also does." If you were blessed with a good relationship with your father perhaps you recall "working" alongside him in the shop or singing with him in the choir or pushing the lawn mower with him. You might remember that no matter what you did, Dad always seemed to make the work you did together turn out well. You might recall the sense of being stronger and more capable with Dad by your side.

If you're a dad then you've seen the other side of the coin. One spring Saturday several years ago, I stood preparing to stain the deck and backyard fence of our townhouse. I had borrowed our neighbors paint gun to make things move along a little faster. All was going according to plan until my oldest son Michael, then just four years old, showed up and, with his most earnest and eager face on, asked if he could help me paint. I was all too familiar with this kind of "help" and I knew it was going to make my job a lot more difficult, but I couldn't say no. I didn't want to say no. I wanted to give my son a chance to work with his Dad just as I had with mine. So, after several hours, we succeeded in painting the fence, the deck, the grass, part of our aluminum siding and one of my neighbors' trees. Was it the easiest way? No. Could I have done it better alone? No doubt. But it was a day that neither of us has forgotten.

Be of good cheer, GOD isn't loading another expectation on you; He is inviting you to participate with Him at his work. It's a heavenly "take your child to work day" invitation.

So what?

So how does all of this discussion impact the knock-down drag-out fight for the souls of the worlds children?

After reading Psalm 68:5-6, the answer should come into focus.

"A father to the fatherless, a defender of widows,

is GOD in his holy dwelling.

GOD sets the lonely in families"

Psalm 68:5-6a

If our Father GOD is a "Father to the fatherless" a "defender of widows" who "places the lonely in families," then we, as his children, his imitators, should be mimicking these traits in our lives.

Is this line of reasoning born out elsewhere in scripture? I believe it is. GOD gives specific instruction for treatment of the fatherless and the widow. His law, as laid out

CHAPTER 4 – GOD IS IN YOUR CORNER SO COME OUT SWINGING!

for us in the Old Testament, is chock-full of commands to care for the fatherless and the widow among us. James repeats these calls in the New Testament when he makes this radical statement.

"Religion that God our Father accepts as pure and faultless is this: to look after orphans and widows in their distress and to keep oneself from being polluted by the world." James 1:27

In the following chapters we will explore what this might look like in your life. We will hear testimonies of men and their families who are engaged in the fight in very real and practical ways and hopefully encourage you to step into the fray.

Chapter 5 - Of Bull Elephants and Shark Wranglers

CHAPTER 5 – OF BULL ELEPHANTS AND SHARK WRANGLERS

To begin unpacking Psalm 68:5-6 we need to first explore what it means to be a "Father to fatherless," and the critical role the church can and must play as the last man standing. We will see how that is reflected in the life of a godly man and, should he be blessed to have one, his family. We will also examine the role for the godly woman and the local Christian congregation in what at first may seem like mostly a "guy thing."

Elephants behaving badly

Those who know me well know that I love a good story, especially a true one and extra-especially one with dangerous animals involved. My mother would tell you that not much has changed in that regard since my childhood. I am hoping that you like them to because I have a couple I'd like to share with you. This first one made headlines back in 1999 when it appeared in a report by CBS news. The tale goes something like this,

In South Africa's Pilanesberg Park, white rhinos began turning up dead in astonishing numbers, nearly forty to be exact. This was alarming and confusing: alarming because it represented 10% of the whole population of white rhinos, and confusing because the deaths hadn't been the result of poaching. The latter was made clear by the fact that the highly valuable ivory horns had not been removed. A little bit of investigation led the park rangers to the culprits, juvenile male elephants. But why? This was not normal behavior for juvenile elephants at all. What could possibly have led them, as was subsequently observed, to form into violent groups and rampage through the park, molesting, tormenting and eventually killing white rhinos? The answer to the question can be found by looking at the history of the park as well as elephant social structure.

For the sake of full disclosure, I am not an expert on elephants, but this story intrigued me so I did some reading. In elephant "culture" the young are raised by the females of the herd until a certain age. We'll call that age adolescence. At that point the male elephants are pushed out of the group and will seek out the older bull elephants of their family (grandfathers, father and uncles presumably) in the wild where they will essentially, "learn what it means to be a bull elephant," which, by the way, does not include murdering rhinos.

Street Thugs of the Savannah

So what went wrong at Pilanesberg? For that answer we need to travel back some twenty years from the time of the rhino killings. In those days another large reserve in South Africa, Kruger National Park, was having an elephant over-population problem. A government veterinarian (it just had to

CHAPTER 5 – OF BULL ELEPHANTS AND SHARK WRANGLERS

be the government right?) developed the ingenious plan to sacrifice the adults, because they were too difficult to move, and instead relocate only the babies. Where to? To Pilanesberg of course.

When these now "fatherless" baby boy elephants reached adolescence; they went out into the wild to look for their male "kinfolk." When there were no bull elephants to be found these youngsters stuck together and formed gangs. Yes, gangs. Interestingly enough, one of the things older bull elephants do for their juvenile counterparts is to discourage them from mating too young. This keeps their testosterone in check and, as a result, diminishes some of their more aggressive impulses. Without older bull elephants to lead the way, the young bulls began mating and seeking to mate at a very young age, stimulating their testosterone levels through the roof and, just like that, dead rhinos and other such mayhem. Sadly, several of these delinquent elephants were put down before someone finally had a stroke of real genius.

Elephant Big Brother Program

Using modified trucks, larger, older bull elephants were trucked in from Kruger Park by rangers. What happened then must have seemed like a miracle. A new hierarchy almost immediately emerged as the older bulls quickly established themselves as dominant over the younger, smaller bulls. Through sparring with the younger elephants, the older bulls successfully discouraged them from being sexually active. This, predictably, lowered testosterone levels and the rhinos, once again, were safe to roam the savannah. In fact, since the big bulls arrived on the scene, not a single rhino has been molested.

Taking a page out of the playbook

Is this so different from what is happening with fatherless children in communities all around the world? It is precisely what we described when we talked about "street activity" and the missing "strong man" in our communities. So what is the lesson here? Fathers are important? Yes. Youth, and boys in particular, are trouble if left alone without supervision? Clearly. We've already established that the "strong man" has been tied up and what the ramifications of that are for our children and society. But this is more than a wild kingdom mirror image of what is happening in our communities and around the world. It is also a road map for how the last man standing, the church of Jesus Christ, could and should respond.

Our neighborhoods are overflowing with fatherless children, both boys and girls, who are in desperate need of interested adults: in need of a provider, protector, teacher and friend. Remember what we said previously, it cannot be just any old mentor but a godly father figure, one who is committed to modeling a Christ centered life, is equipped for

CHAPTER 5 – OF BULL ELEPHANTS AND SHARK WRANGLERS

the battle and one who is engaged in actively teaching the truth within the context of a loving and safe relationship.

These children are waiting for the old bull elephants to come and put things straight. Whether they realize it or not, these "youth gone wild" are desperate for an old bull to come along and say, "Whoa there boys, not the rhino's. That's not how we roll. You follow me and I'll show you the way it's done."

Fatherless girls need to hear an old bull say, "Sweetheart, you are precious in GOD's eyes. You are loved. Don't let those young bulls fool you into giving away your heart. Don't throw yourself at them. Give them time to mature. Stick with me and I'll protect you and value you for who you are, not what you can do for me."

Several studies published over the last twenty years have focused on children identified as "students at risk" for behaviors ranging from out-of-wedlock pregnancy, drug use, and alcohol abuse. The students who did not get involved in those behaviors identified one common reason; someone took a personal interest in them in such a way that they felt loved and connected. Children at-risk are in need of some old bulls to ride in and say to Satan and his workers, as Jesus did in Matthew 18:6, "If anyone causes one of these little ones to stumble, it would be better for them to have a large millstone hung around their neck and to be drowned in the depths of the sea." Can it make a difference? Can you make a difference? Let's see.

Eduardo continued

...When we left Eduardo he was serving out his time in the infamous FEBEM juvenile prison system of Brazil, never hearing from a single "friend," his only visitor being his mother. But then he got a letter that would change everything. The letter, came from a an old P.E. teacher from his grade school years, Marcelo, and was accompanied by a photograph of the two of them together with some other boys from one of the many schools he had passed through in his childhood. Marcelo wrote that he had heard from some friends of the trouble Eduardo had gotten himself into and let him know that he was praying for him and would like to catch up with him upon his release. It was a simple letter, but it was also the only letter Eduardo would get from anyone throughout his 18-month sentence.

The day of his release came and it wasn't long after getting home that his so called, "friends" came to welcome him back. Their first order of business was to invite him on a home invasion they were planning in the coming days. He accepted. In the mean time he thought he should at least track down Marcelo, this P.E. teacher who he still couldn't believe remembered him, and thank him for the kind letter. He found Marcelo, thanked him and, after a little chitchat, was ready to go back home, mission accomplished. But then Marcelo

CHAPTER 5 – OF BULL ELEPHANTS AND SHARK WRANGLERS

invited him to come out to a party with some youth from his church. Eduardo was leery of going to a "church" thing, but Marcelo assured him it was purely social and not a worship service. He accepted, completely missing that the night of the party was the same night as the planned robbery.

Attending that party with Marcelo, Eduardo was taken aback by the other youth he met. They were different. The way they talked to each other and to him was completely foreign to him, but he liked it. The next day his "friends" came around and asked why he had blown them off and not shown up as planned. Eduardo made some excuses and rescheduled for another night the following week. The day of that robbery Marcelo paid an unexpected visit to Eduardo and invited him to join them again for a night out. This time Eduardo jumped at the chance, completely forgetting that he was "double booking" himself yet again. Once more he had a great time with Marcelo and his new friends and was more and more intrigued by what made them so different.

The next morning the old crew showed up at his home, even more frustrated with being dissed another time. Eduardo wasn't so sure of the sincerity of his apology this time, but rescheduled once more just the same. The day came and this time it was Eduardo calling Marcelo to ask if he could please come to a worship service being held for the youth at a local church that night. It was the last time Eduardo would schedule a robbery, because that night, as Marcelo shared the good news of Jesus with the youth gathered together, GOD stole Eduardo's heart for good.

Soon after, Marcelo introduced Eduardo to Patricia and me at an Open Arms outreach project and we got him plugged in as a volunteer, teaching hip-hop dance to the kids. Marcelo, Patricia and I have been walking with Eduardo ever since. He has lived in our home, sharing a room with our boys, when things were going badly in his. He has shared meals and holidays with our family. Eduardo has gone on to go to college, marry his sweetheart, plant (at the time of this writing) three Open Arms outreach projects, share his testimony all over Brazil, begin an outreach back into the same juvenile facility he spent time in, and lead untold numbers of children and youth to Christ. Eduardo says today, "After about three months of resisting the temptation of returning to drugs and crime, my so-called "friends" stopped coming around. Had it not been for my newfound faith in Jesus and friends from Open Arms, I don't think I would have made it."

An interesting footnote to this story of Eduardo is that, on one particular evening soon after his conversion, he was invited with some of the other church youth to a meeting at a house belonging to the family of one of the girls in the youth group, one of his new best friends. As they arrived at the house Eduardo's jaw dropped. It was the very same house he and his crew had planned to rob the day he went to jail, the day a voice inside him said, "Not this house." He knew now whom that voice belonged to.

CHAPTER 5 – OF BULL ELEPHANTS AND SHARK WRANGLERS

Sound Scary?

"At-risk children in my house? Drugs dealers and thieves? Juvenile detention centers? Are you crazy? That is the kind of thing best left for professionals, missionaries or folks without their own family to care for. Besides, in this country you can get sued for looking the wrong way at a child. The risks are just too great. What if I just write a check?"

As the President of a non-profit organization that survives on the giving heart of GOD's people, I would say, yes, please do. Better yet, you, your family, your business and your church could purpose to become regular financial partners with an organization, like Open Arms Worldwide, that is working to get more "bull elephants" out into the places where children have been left most vulnerable. But, if you stop there you are missing out. Is it dangerous and risky? Absolutely. But with great risk comes great reward.

Do Not Fear

That leads me to my second animal story. This one took place in the warm gulf coast waters of Florida in 2001 and was picked up and reported by most major television news networks at the time. A man was relaxing at the beach with some relatives when he heard screams and looked to see a pool of blood forming around his nephew who was standing in the shallow water. A seven-foot long, 250-pound bull shark had a firm hold on the boy and wasn't letting go.

Shark Wrangler

The uncle jumped into the water, as most of us would, and, taking hold of the sharks' tail, pulled the animal away from the boy. The shark released, but had taken the child's arm just below the shoulder. He was losing a lot of blood as his aunt began caring for him on shore. At that point the uncle would have been perfectly justified in releasing his hold on the shark and returning to the safety of shore to care for his nephew, but that would have to wait, there were other children still in the water. Holding on tightly to that tail, he wrestled the beast, which was all the while trying to turn on him, up on to the beach where a park ranger shot it with his 9mm service pistol. The boys' arm was retrieved and reattached, and the immediate danger to the other children in the water was removed.

Substitute "Strong Man"

Brothers, we all know it is our GOD given duty as men to care for our own children, to protect them, to fight off the sharks of this world and guide our children on the narrow path that leads to life. But as Christian men we have a call that goes beyond just our own little ones. "This is how we know what love is: Jesus Christ laid down his life for us. And we

CHAPTER 5 – OF BULL ELEPHANTS AND SHARK WRANGLERS

ought to lay down our lives for our brothers." 1 John 3:16. It is not enough to hide with our children, or the children of the church on shore, within our homes, our safe neighborhoods or the walls of the church building, when there are still children in the water with the sharks.

Ladies, are you laboring with the men in your life as a team to pull more children away from the sharks, like the aunt in our story, binding up the wounds of one child while he goes back for more? Jesus Christ laid down his life for us, as a substitute. When the "strong man" in the life of a child has been removed we, as Christ imitators, the last men standing, have the privilege to step into the gap, in the name of the Savior, as a substitute and sure up the walls in the life of that young person.

Does that sound scary? Sure it does. But "perfect love drives out fear" (1 John 4:18). If this is a mission from our Father, and it is, then we must trust in the words that GOD said to Joshua and to all those warriors who would follow, "Have I not commanded you? Be strong and courageous. Do not be afraid; do not be discouraged, for the LORD your GOD will be with you wherever you go." (Joshua 1:9).

Raphael the fearless

"Truly I tell you, unless you change and become like little **children**, you will never enter the kingdom of heaven." (Matthew 18:3)

Early on in our work in Brazil we made a lot of rookie mistakes. One in particular led to a wonderful story of the fearless faith of a child. I think it might just encourage the shark wrangler hidden within you.

We had begun our first outreach using a building belonging to a little church. As we reorganized to make space for our material we encountered a room full to the ceiling with used clothes. Clothing had been collected for a bazaar and these were the leftovers. The clothes were in good condition, but no one was quite sure what to do with them. So after getting permission from the pastor, we set a date to take the clothes and distribute them in a favela (slum neighborhood) adjoining the neighborhood where the church was located. On a typically balmy Brazilian summer afternoon we loaded the clothing into the back of our pick-up truck and headed out. My two boys, Michael (9) and Raphael (7) were riding along, as well as Pastor Tiago, my friend Marcelo, and another boy from the outreach, Adriano.

CHAPTER 5 – OF BULL ELEPHANTS AND SHARK WRANGLERS

A Just Cause

As we pulled to a stop in the neighborhood we were immediately approached by curious children and then adults asking what we were doing. When they realized we were giving things away, the word went out and in an instant a sea of humanity surrounded us. People pushed and shouted as we tried to distribute the clothes in some semblance of order. About that time the door of the pick-up opened (I had forgotten to lock the door in the confusion) and some children jumped in and started grabbing at whatever they could find. My soccer ball went first and then one of them grabbed my handsaw and took off up the street. My youngest boy Raphael saw the whole thing and yelled to me, "Dad, that boy stole your saw!" I told him we had bigger problems and that we just needed to lock the doors now so that my wallet wasn't next. He insisted, "But that wasn't a donation! That's stealing and it's wrong!" Again, I told him to forget about it. Next thing I know, there goes my little boy, barefoot, up the street, through the favela after the saw. He didn't hear me when I called to him so I asked Adriano to tail him and make sure he didn't get into any trouble.

After a few minutes I was getting worried. The throng began to subside as the last of the clothing was carted off. Where was my son? I looked up and my heart jumped as I saw Raphael walking back toward the truck...with a triumphant look on his face and my saw in his hand. As scary as that was for a dad, I learned a lesson that day. **When our mission is just and godly we cannot let fear stop us.**

The Great Claim & The Great Promise

What could be scarier than going on a rescue mission into a hostile world in the name of Christ? Most of us are familiar with the Great Commission as recorded for us in Matthew chapter 28. In this famous scene Jesus commissioned the disciples, and those disciples not yet born, to go into the world and share the gospel with the nations. What most of us forget is that there are bookends to the Great Commission, namely the Great Claim and the Great Promise. Let's take a look.

"Then Jesus came to them and said, ***"All authority in heaven and on earth has been given to me [the Great Claim]. Therefore*** *go and make disciples of all nations, baptizing them in the name of the Father and of the Son and of the Holy Spirit, and teaching them to obey everything I have commanded you.* ***And surely I am with you always, to the very end of the age.[the Great Promise]"***

Number one, Jesus first claims the authority, all authority, to say what he is about to say. No one in their right mind charges into battle on the orders of a Private 1st Class. It just doesn't happen. We want to know authority backs up the orders. Jesus has been given all power that exists, in heaven

CHAPTER 5 – OF BULL ELEPHANTS AND SHARK WRANGLERS

and on earth. This command comes from the highest of all authorities.

After Jesus lays this very scary battle plan on us, he follows it up with a promise. "Not only do I have the authority to send you on this mission, but I myself will be fighting along with you every step of the way." Do you believe him?

Lucas continued

When we left Lucas he was beginning to attend a new school, a gathering of the worst of the worst from the city's overburdened school system. Their first "field trip" would change his life forever... Lucas' class would be going to a local swim school that had been contracted by the city to teach swim lessons. A shark wrangler by the nickname, "Zinho," is the school's owner as well as a former coach for Brazil's Olympic program and a follower of Jesus Christ. He was on hand that first day. He looked on as these unruly delinquents plunged willy-nilly into the pool. One of them in particular caught his well-trained eye. This smallish, Afro-Brazilian boy dove in headfirst and, although he had no idea how to swim, he seemed to be at home in the water. Zinho called Lucas from the pool and asked if he would like to learn to be a competitive swimmer. Lucas wasn't sure what was involved, but he sure liked the pool and figured it was a good chance to spend more time there.

LAST MAN STANDING

In those days our organization, Open Arms, was also beginning to lead Bible-based, civic and moral education classes in Lucas' new school. Because my sons were also swimming at Zinho's academy, he and I talked a lot together about the school and about Lucas. We agreed that Open Arms would start a Bible study with the children on the swim team. Zinho recruited an older gentleman from his church to also meet with Lucas for one-on-one discipleship every week. Lucas began to split his time between our home and the swim school, where Zinho had made up a room for him.

It was a bumpy road, as Lucas had no experience with limits or personal discipline of any kind. His brothers were drug users and well-known thieves and tough guys in one of the most notorious neighborhoods of the city (coincidentally one of Lucas' brothers was incarcerated with Eduardo from our earlier story). His mother had no interest in caring for him but held on to legal guardianship in order to receive a small pension that was intended for his care. He once asked me tearfully, "Why did GOD give me such a terrible family? Why couldn't I have a family like yours? Why couldn't Maikinho and Rapha (my two boys) be my brothers?"

Lucas still has a lot of hurt to overcome, but in the context of a safe, healthy relationship with godly men and their families, Lucas gave his own life to Jesus.

Today Lucas talks of college and eventually a wife and family. He told me recently, "I will never quit now. I know what I want and I know what GOD wants of me." For Lucas,

CHAPTER 5 – OF BULL ELEPHANTS AND SHARK WRANGLERS

the psalmists' words are his own, "Though my father and mother forsake me, the LORD will receive me." (Psalm 27:10).

The Spirit of GOD works through the lives of men committed to be fathers to the fatherless. It's time for the shark wranglers and bull elephants of the Church to stand up and step out. It can and will make difference in the lives of the children you touch.

Chapter 6 - "A defender of widows"

CHAPTER 6 – A DEFENDER OF WIDOWS

Stephen, Beth & Tyler

Beth and her husband Stephen had found a church family where they felt at home, cared for, and free to serve Christ with their gifts. Some five years earlier they had adopted their son Tyler from Guatemala when he was just 9 months old and this little church in North Carolina had lots of young families and children Tyler's age. Things were good, but unseen storm clouds were mounting.

Stephen had struggled with a staph infection in his arm back in 2009 that required surgery and then another infection in 2011 that affected his face, eye and throat. In both cases, strong doses of antibiotic seemed to do the trick. It was almost Thanksgiving in 2011 when Stephen's arm started to act up again. He shrugged it off and opted not to go to the doctor. In the following days the pain spread up his arm to his shoulder and then he began to have flu like symptoms. It was flu season so again, he self-medicated, shrugged it off and didn't go to the doctor. Thanksgiving Day was filled with lots of soup and liquids as Stephen struggled to keep anything down. By Friday evening things had deteriorated with vomiting, diarrhea and a fever, which had spiked dangerously. His arm was also swollen and red. He was having difficulty breathing and holding up his head as Beth and her in-laws wrestled him into the car and rushed him to the hospital.

LAST MAN STANDING

Doctors and nurses rushed around trying to determine what the problem was while Stephen's condition continued to deteriorate. Their pastor, Mike, arrived while they were still awaiting a bed. This seemed to lift Stephen's spirits, but the news from the staff was not what Beth had hoped for. She was told her husband would likely not make it through the night. As they wheeled him off to the ICU he uttered his last words to her.

Doctors discovered that Stephen was suffering with Toxic Shock Syndrome brought on by an untreated Strep A virus infection. Despite heroic efforts by the doctors, there was nothing more that could be done. His internal tissues had been so badly ravaged by the infection that even an amputation of all his limbs would be to no avail. The family and the church family gathered at the hospital. Young Tyler went in to say goodbye to his dad, telling him to "go be with GOD now."

Along with Beth and Stephen's parents and close relatives, at his bedside stood three men who would go on to play critical roles in her life and the life of her young son Tyler. These were their Pastors, Mike, Matt, and Tim.

Stephen went home to be with the Lord on December 5, 2011, but he did not leave his Beth and Tyler alone. He had invested wisely for the future of his wife and son.

"Stephen was the most loving, generous and kind person I ever met. He loved life. His childlike qualities are what attracted me to him in the first place. He enjoyed every second he was on this

earth. He loved people and helping people. I know that our church saw that in him the second they met him. We started helping the church from the second week we went." – Beth

Who is the "widow" among us?

The word, "fatherless" appears forty-one times in scripture and most often together with another word not so commonly used in western culture today, that being the word "widow." Widows are inextricably linked in scripture to the fatherless as an equally vulnerable group of people. The link between the two is also very often biological as the child of a widow is by definition, "fatherless."

In Bible times and in many parts of the developing world today, disease and war often end the lives of young men prematurely, making the issue of widows, their social vulnerability and that of their now "fatherless" children of great concern. Although less common, we do, as Beth's story illustrates, still encounter young widows in our times. How we handle these situations is often not something Jesus' brother James would be proud of.

"Pure religion and undefiled before our GOD and Father is this, to visit the fatherless and widows in their affliction, and to keep oneself unspotted from the world." James 1:27 ASV.

All too often, after the initial outpouring of compassion and assistance that often come when someone loses their husband, people begin to drop away. They are busy with their own lives and being around a widow just reminds them of the person that has been lost. No one wants to dwell on that. To their other married friends and church family the widow may begin to seem like a third wheel without her husband. Whether it is conscious or not, people tend to draw away. It is the rare family and rare church that ministers to the widow over the long haul.

Our three heroes in Beth's story are trying to buck the trend and be the Psalm 68 Church, the last man standing. As of the writing of this book Beth's loss is less than a year old and she is struggling desperately to cope with this new life that was thrust on her.

"Now life is very lonely. I miss having a man around the house." "Someone to hold me and tell me everything is going to be okay, someone to talk to, to help me parent Tyler. I have to do the grass by myself, the bills, the shopping, the coupon cutting, bath time, story time, fighting with my son to get him into bed." "I worry every single day about Tyler and if what I am doing is the right thing for him. I never wanted to be a single mother. I loved being married to my husband."

As hard as this is on her, Beth's pastors, and the body of believers they lead, are sacrificially stepping into the gap.

"I have been asking [Pastor] Mike and he has been helping me understand the Bible. I have been reading about widows and how I am supposed to live. He is meeting my spiritual goals together with Cheri and Matt and Anna. I feel the closest to them and feel

CHAPTER 6 – A DEFENDER OF WIDOWS

like they really help me to understand and talk with GOD. I feel like it is very important to learn as much as I can. I really want to understand heaven, GOD and life in general so I can serve." "The church continues to help me financially. They continue to come over and fix things or do anything they can to help."

Beth and Tyler have a long way to go, and it won't be easy, but because of godly people doing what the church is called to do, there is hope. Tyler has men in the church to model godly manhood just as Stephen would have. Beth is growing closer to the Lord through the care of her brothers and sisters in Christ.

Correcting a Blind Spot

In developed nations the casual observer might point out that the widow with young children, like Beth, is much less common. This is true in the technical sense. Praise GOD that in this day and age our young men are living long lives and tragedies like the one that has befallen Beth are more and more rare. But before we jump to that final conclusion and assume that widows are a mostly third world issue, I think we must take a closer look at western society and make sure we are not suffering from a blind spot that a small change in perspective would correct.

The functional widow

What is a widow really? A woman whose husband has died? Yes, but more generally, as I stated in an earlier chapter, it is a woman who does not have a husband, or father for her children, to serve as protector, provider, teacher and friend to that family. With today's globalized cultural epidemics of rampant out-of-wedlock birth, divorce, drug related incarceration and social welfare dependence; I suggest we need to expand our definition of a widow to include single mothers.

Although they may receive some financial assistance from the father of their children and perhaps share custody, the impact of the "strong man" in that family unit has been greatly diminished if not completely cancelled out. Single moms, whether by death, divorce or abandonment, are, for all intents and purposes, widows. As we saw in the downward spiral of fatherlessness in poor communities, single mothers are forced to fill both parenting roles. This, more often than not, leads to families falling into "survival" mode, where the lower level needs, or as Maslow put it, physiological needs such as food, shelter and clothing, push aside the higher level needs of faith, community, and character education. Children are less supervised as the remaining parent seeks to provide resources; they have fewer positive role models for family life and are thus made more vulnerable to the schemes of the world. The results are predictable and well documented.

CHAPTER 6 – A DEFENDER OF WIDOWS

If then, we were to replace the term "single mother" with the term "widow," it would become painfully obvious that we as the church of Jesus in general have an even more dismal record of obedience to GOD's command to be "defenders" of the widows among us than we first imagined.

In her article, "The Church and the Single Mom," Jennifer Barnes Maggio says this about the state of affairs for "functional widows" and their fatherless children in the church.

"The single mom is one of the fastest-growing sects of our population, so why have we, the church, ignored them for so long? According to the U.S. Census Bureau's article "Custodial Mothers and Fathers and Their Child Support" released in November 2007, there are more than 13 million across the United States with 27 percent living in poverty and 24 percent receiving government assistance. Many of these single moms come from generations of single moms with no hope of ever breaking this cycle. Currently, 78 percent of our prison population comes from a single-parent home, according to the Index of Leading Cultural Indicators. A study released in March 2007 by University of Pennsylvania's School of Medicine found that almost 50 percent of the single-parent homes have some form of sexual abuse.

For far too long the church has run from the single mom. Some studies suggest as many as 67 percent of single moms currently do not attend church — many citing fear of being judged as key. Of course, we offer them food when they are hungry. We may occasionally perform a home repair or provide toys at Christmas.

LAST MAN STANDING

However, do we stop there? Dare we open a Sunday school class exclusively for single moms? A Bible study? Or even a full-scale ministry?"

That is pretty convicting stuff. Out of our often well-placed fear of promoting divorce or out-of-wedlock sexual relations, we have taken the position that this category of "widow" among us somehow deserves, whether in whole or in part, the situation in which she finds herself.

Let's assume for a second, for the sake of argument, that she is entirely at fault for her marital status. So what? Since when do we tell someone who is suffering the results of sin in their lives that they are un-deserving of Christ's love? Who gave us that right? On what grounds do we think it is acceptable to not reach out to her and her children in order to call them to Christ and help them break what can easily become a generational cycle of broken homes and lives?

"For while we were yet sinners, Christ died for us."
(Romans 5:8)

Someone once told me that mercy is not getting what we DO deserve and grace is getting the blessing that we DO NOT deserve. What **is** the gospel if not the un-deserved mercy and grace of GOD? How many of us think we "deserve" either?

The life of the single mother is difficult enough without cutting her off from the one entity that has the answers for her fears and her hopelessness. Why are we turning our backs

CHAPTER 6 – A DEFENDER OF WIDOWS

when we should be drawing close? These single mom's and their children need the church and its families to support them, to model healthy, godly marriage to them, to give them an opportunity to see Jesus in action in their own lives through His people.

Is your church a Psalm 68 church when it comes to widows and single mothers? Are you? There are as many ways to bless and defend the widow as your imagination allows. We need simply to make the decision to imitate our Father and He will show us the way.

Chapter 7 - "He places the lonely in families"

CHAPTER 7 – HE PLACES THE LONELY IN FAMILIES

Mariana continued

A loving father, a godly friend, or a safe place to just be a child were all foreign concepts until the day a concerned city health worker took an interest and sought out help...

When Mariana arrived at the Open Arms outreach that day in 2007 we had no idea what to expect. She was part of a group of about seven children who had been referred to us by a concerned nurse from the health clinic that serves Mariana's neighborhood. She and her comrades weren't sure what to expect either and so they began on day one to test the boundaries. It was mayhem! At one point, in desperation, I took the lot of them to the library where I could speak privately and said something like this, "You all are here because someone cares about you and wants to give you a chance at hope and a future. I am here because Jesus loves me and He loves you. So you can try to test me and push as much as you want, but I'm not giving up on you because GOD never gave up on me."

It would be a beautiful testimony if that little talk fixed everything, but it would take a lot more than talk to convince Mariana that what I was saying was true. It would take visits to her home to meet her mother and sisters, helping out with groceries when things were tight, taking her to youth camp with us, attending school events with her, and hundreds of other little gestures to show her that we loved her and cared about her in Jesus' name.

More and more Mariana connected the things we taught her from the Bible with the way we loved her every day, until one day she believed those words I had spoken to her way back when we first met. My daughter, Gabriela, who was five years old at the time, sat with me and Mariana in a little room at the outreach where we were videotaping interviews with the children about Open Arms and what it meant in their lives. When I asked Mariana to tell me who Jesus was to her, she just looked at me as though she didn't understand the question. I'm not sure if it was the way I phrased the question or what, but she was stumped. Before I could try to re-phrase, Gabriela jumped in and began to explain to Mariana what the good news about Jesus is and how wonderful Jesus was to her. Her five year olds' presentation was so simple and genuine that I had nothing to add other than to ask Mariana if she wanted to give her life and heart to Jesus. She did and so she prayed with us and that was that.

In the following year one of Mariana's sisters, who had been part of a car theft ring, also received Jesus as her savior and began to take her four little ones to church. She found a real job and moved into a house of her own. I had the opportunity to visit with Mariana's brother in juvenile detention where, upon hearing of his sister's decision, he asked for prayer and talked about his desire to repent. Mariana now at age 14 is an apprentice volunteer and her story is still unfolding, but I am confident that He who began a good work in her life will carry it on to completion. Mariana has a very large family but she is part of an even bigger family now. I interviewed Mariana recently for another video and when I asked again, "Who is Jesus to you?" she replied without missing a beat, "He is my father. He is everything to me."

Placing the lonely in families

There is no denying the facts; we are called to sincerely imitate our Father, as Jesus did, and we cannot claim ignorance as to His character or the work He is about. What then are we to do? You might say, "I'm not Superman. I can't save the world on my own." I agree. No you're not and no you can't. But we can make a difference in one person's, or one family's, life when we act together as a church and as a family. Our GOD, "places the lonely in _families_."

Since before time began, GOD the Father is complete within his family, along with the Son and the Holy Spirit. He did not need to create mankind to keep him company or to fulfill some unmet longing within his self. GOD did not need to become involved with us when we began to go off track. He was not obligated to protect, provide, teach or befriend us. He most certainly did not need to send his own Son to be sacrificed for our sake. But he **did** do all those things. Incredibly, he has gone even further by giving us the right to be "adopted as sons" and made us "co-heirs" with his own true Son. That is astonishing. Are there families really being "imitators" of GOD at that level?

Let me count the ways!

I am sure you know parents who, after having their biological children, have chosen to adopt as well. Many of these parents have adopted children that are older or less "attractive" candidates for some other reason. We have had the privilege of meeting one family who, after having four children, decided to adopt seven brothers and sisters! This is probably the clearest expression of God's heart as Father to fatherless, but it would be a mistake to think that if you are not called to adoption then you have no role to play. There are many ways God can use your family in this fight.

Maybe you've seen the 2009 film, "The Blind Side," based on the life of NFL star Michael Oher and starring Quinton Aaron, Sandra Bullock and Tim McGraw. If you have not, you should. This family took a young person, they barely knew, into their home, into their family (potentially putting their other two children at risk), fed him, housed him, did homework with him, eventually bought a car for him and helped him get into a good school; all things that they also did for their own children.

If you saw the film, perhaps your gut reaction was, after drying your eyes, "Beautiful story, but that's a once in a lifetime thing" or "That family was rich, we couldn't afford to do that." If so, you should take a minute right now and Google some other names in the sports world like, Todd Williams, Keith Bulluck, Marcus Dixon, Patrick Willis, and Jeremy Maclin. All of these young men have strikingly similar stories to that of Michael Oher. A family reached out to them when they were alone and in need of help. A family opened their home and their hearts and changed their lives for the better. Then there is the story of James Robert Kennedy, immortalized in the 2003 film, "Radio." While not a child chronologically, "Radio," with his developmental challenges, was in every other way a fatherless and vulnerable young person. What high school football coach Harold Jones and his family did for him was a perfect picture of God's love for us.

These good news stories are not only in the sports arena either. Every day regular families are allowing themselves to be used as conduits for GOD's love, but not nearly enough of them to meet the growing need. Why not? After all, it sounds noble and romantic. For the ladies, your mother hen instinct makes this almost second nature. For the guys, the warrior within you longs to be a "savior" and rescuer. These are good and godly drives that, when tempered by the knowledge that we do nothing apart from GOD (John 5:19), will be a blessing in the Father's hands.

Reality Check

At the same time I want to encourage you to embrace your role as "last man standing," I also must warn you that it is anything but easy. Just as war often appears noble and romantic until you have been there, the reality of stepping into the gap for the fatherless can be a rude awakening for those unprepared. Opening your home, exposing your children to the harsh realities of a fallen world, having unexpected visitors at all hours, extra mouths to feed, sacrificing family/couple/me time to mentor a child from a broken home, or having someone new at a family event, are all challenges associated with living a Psalm 68 lifestyle and can't be taken lightly.

> "They've got big hearts. To take somebody from my neighborhood into your house? Nobody does that. I don't think I'd even do that. I'd help you out, but with a daughter and with all the violence and drugs where I come from ... they didn't have to do that. I owe a lot to them." – Michael Oher (interview in USA Today by Jarrett Bell)

This path is full of pitfalls and frustration, but if we fail to be that lifeline when GOD gives us opportunity, we will miss the blessings.

> "We think GOD sent him [Michael Oher] to us. Earthly explanations don't make sense." – Sean Tuohy (interview in USA Today by Jarrett Bell)

CHAPTER 7 – HE PLACES THE LONELY IN FAMILIES

So what could this look like in your life? Are we all to have fatherless children living on our sofa beds? Before you freak out, let's take a look at a few examples and see how GOD might move your family or church to take similar steps.

Zinho

Remember our friend Zinho? Born Elias Macruz Filho, "Zinho" as most everyone knows him, is a swim coach and owner, with his wife Margaret, of a small swim school in Brazil. After going through his own hard times as a youth trying to study and excel as an athlete and suffering with family problems along the way, Zinho, through hard work and his faith in Jesus, achieved a certain level of success in his life. He is not rich but he has a business, is well respected for his coaching achievements and should be thinking about a comfortable retirement. Instead, he stubbornly continues to find underprivileged children who want to swim and encourages them to dream big, to work hard in the pool and at their studies; all the while sharing with them the hope of faith in Jesus that changed his life. He helps them get scholarships to better schools, often finds jobs for their single mothers, and mobilizes his paying clients to give a little more so he can provide extra meals to supplement the poor nutrition of many of these children. It is not uncommon to find him in his kitchen cooking or making smoothies for a table full of swimmers while he goes on about the importance of his faith in Jesus.

Most of these children go home, but some, like Lucas in our earlier story, have become part of the family, taking vacations with them, participating in family events and having birthday party's right there in their home.

Not long ago, after some frustrating financial moments, I asked Zinho why he didn't just sell the school, which sits on a very well located and valuable piece of land, and move to an apartment on the beach. His children are grown and doing well, why put up with the headaches?

He said, "GOD picked me up, dusted me off, saved me and forgave me. He gave me all this and I have purposed in my heart to honor him with it. If I can be a part of changing the life of just one child it will be worth it."

Zinho is an old school coach, and old school father, and has a lot of rough edges, but he and his family are committed to being in GOD's will.

Nancy

Nancy is a lawyer, has raised her own children, and lives comfortably with her husband in the suburbs of Washington DC. She is active in her church, has donated her time on the boards of several not-for-profit organizations and gives generously. Nancy has reached a time in her life when she and her husband should be enjoying their time together and coasting. They have run the race. But when a young

CHAPTER 7 – HE PLACES THE LONELY IN FAMILIES

couple they knew got the disastrous news that the husband had a rare and deadly cancer, their priorities changed.

This young couple and their small child quickly ran through any savings they had with experimental treatments in an effort to save his life. The battle had its up and downs with the disease being fought into remission for a time, but once it came back with a vengeance the young family eventually lost their home.

Nancy and her husband could have done a lot of things to help, but what they did do amazed me. Their furnished basement became home for this family. Once again the sound of little feet, not heard since her children, now adults, ran the halls, was back. Nancy walked with this young wife and mother through the last days of her husband's life and continues to shelter and mentor this young widow and her fatherless child. More amazing is that she doesn't seem to see her behavior as exceptional. She is only doing what she sees her Father in heaven doing.

A Bible Church in Northern VA

When the congregation of a thriving Northern Virginia Church moved into their new home in the town of Sterling and began looking for ways they could make a positive impact on their new community, they never imagined what the Lord had prepared for them. Hidden away in one of the most affluent counties in the nation, lies one elementary school where last year 85% of the children attending were from families living at or below the poverty line. Within this little school there are children from fifty different countries, speaking ten different languages. Poverty, broken families, and illiteracy, combined with insufficient funding, are all major problems facing the embattled but dedicated teaching staff.

Some church leaders approached the school Principal and asked, "How can we help you? We don't know what we can do or if you even want us to do anything, but we are here and we want to know what we can do to make your community a better place." The principal was reluctant at first and asked why they would want to take this on. Their response was honest and straightforward. "We need to obey what our Lord has called us to do and that is to show love to our neighbors. We don't want to throw it [our faith] in your face, but we do need to be obedient." After thinking it through the Principal replied, "We don't need volunteers. We don't want your people in our school, but we do need some help financially."

Not the most encouraging beginning, but for several months the church provided consistent, faithful help with a summer food program and provision of school supplies. Some of the teachers mentioned that the children couldn't focus before lunch due to hunger. The church stepped in and provided snack and fruit bars in plastic containers so the children could be given a morning snack. A teacher appreciation program was started in order to bless and

CHAPTER 7 – HE PLACES THE LONELY IN FAMILIES

encourage the staff. A book drive provided half a dozen books for each child in the school. As a result of these efforts the Principal's confidence level rose and his heart warmed.

Today the doors of the school are open to a homework buddies program where volunteers from the church are in the classroom assisting children who are learning to read, write and do basic math. One motivated volunteer teacher is even doing tutoring house calls in the community and another man has chosen to work over-time in order to take off from work every Wednesday afternoon to be a homework buddy. About 70 children from the school attended a kid's summer day camp the church held at the end of the school year.

"We don't want to take over their school. They have a great thing going on there. We don't want to mess that up, but we do want to help them make it better."

It is a simple thing to do and they are seeing fruit. Many of the children and their families are attending the church, teachers are being won over by the love of Christ as it's lived out by the volunteers, hearts are being opened, and children's lives are being impacted for eternity.

Edgar & Vera

Edgar runs a sugar cane juice stand downtown and Vera works in a furniture store. This godly couple lives a mile from a small children's shelter run by their city government in the interior of Brazil. While the little children at the shelter are often adopted, not too many people are willing to adopt an older child. Adoption bureaucracy is such that many families shy away from even trying.

Having already raised two fine sons of their own, Edgar and Vera took it upon themselves, through an arrangement with the shelter, to become mentors for some of the adolescent and teenage girls there. They have them for dinner, allow them to spend weekends with them at their farmhouse outside of town, and take them to church and youth group functions. They are modeling a godly Christian marriage and family to children who otherwise would most likely be doomed to repeat the mistakes of their parents. Edgar and Vera are standing in the gap for the fatherless.

Paul & Joan

Paul and Joan are veterans at investing in the lives of children. They have three fine boys of their own and are diehard volunteers in their church's children's programs. But that hasn't stopped them from opening their home and their hearts for even more children.

For several year's they have participated in a program that matches children from tough, inner-city situations with families in the country. For two weeks these youngsters live under their roof as part of their family. They share meals, outings, worship services, and family prayer times together.

CHAPTER 7 – HE PLACES THE LONELY IN FAMILIES

It's not all roses. According to Joan, "It is usually either the longest or fastest two weeks of our year. We are always either completely worn out or wishing we had more time together." It may only be two weeks, but it makes an impression on the lives of young people that could change the course of their future.

Michael

Michael has a solid marriage, three young sons and a successful business in Northern Virginia. He coaches various youth sports teams and is a pillar in his local church. By all accounts he is a godly man, but when Michael began to get involved at his oldest son's high school he discovered that GOD had something more for him.

Michael was shocked to find out how many of the young people at this high school in an affluent community are fatherless. Understanding the critical role a godly father plays and what his absence means for the life of a child, the situation continued to weigh on his heart until a chance meeting with the school's principal at a church worship service where he took the opportunity to open up his heart. What happened next was not a big program or endless meetings, but two men of GOD choosing to act. Today they are actively mentoring a group of boys from that high school, helping them with homework, taking them to church, and looking for more men and families to join them so that every fatherless child there has access to someone who can share truth with them in a safe, loving relationship.

The variety of ways that you can be a part of GOD's work of placing the lonely in families and being a father to the fatherless are vast. I have had the privilege of meeting people who have taken young single parent families under their wing, befriending them, inviting them for holiday dinners, Bible studies, or even family vacations. There are women who have befriended a single mother, helping her to cope with the challenges of raising children alone and being a trusted advisor and mentor.

We have known people who routinely "adopt" lonely college students who are far from home. In our home it is not uncommon to have young "house guests" for weeks or months at a time. Another friend of ours ended up discipling several troubled youth from his neighborhood after some of them saw him practicing with a heavy bag in his garage and asked if he would teach them boxing. I have met Christian men of all ages who are stepping into their communities as coaches and mentors and Boy Scout leaders, volunteer tutors and more.

There are churches who have caught this vision and set up mentoring programs for schools in at-risk communities, partnering individuals and families from their congregations with the fatherless and "widows" in their own backyard. One well-known congregation in the United States has committed

CHAPTER 7 – HE PLACES THE LONELY IN FAMILIES

to raising up families to meet **all** of the foster care needs in their county!

The point here is that the how is just details. Every family is differently gifted and churches are differently positioned, but the important thing, as the "last man standing," is that we live out a Psalm 68 lifestyle, that we work alongside this GOD of ours who is a "Father to the fatherless and defender of widows," who "places the lonely in families."

"He has saved us and called us to a holy life—not because of anything we have done but because of his own purpose and grace. This grace was given us in Christ Jesus before the beginning of time," 2 Timothy 1:9 NIV

"Whoever heard me spoke well of me,

and those who saw me commended me,

because I rescued the poor who cried for help,

and the fatherless who had none to assist them.

The one who was dying blessed me;

I made the widow's heart sing." Job 29:11-13 NIV

There are children waiting. What will be said of us?

Chapter 8 - Open Hearts, Open Arms

CHAPTER 8 – OPEN HEARTS, OPEN ARMS

Being the "last man standing," a father to fatherless, a family for the lonely, and stepping into the breach to rebuild the walls where the "strong man" has been taken down, are all GOD sized tasks. But when we work alongside our Father and in fellowship with our family and our brothers and sisters in Christ, all things are possible. As an encouragement to you, I would like to close here; in the most engaging way I can, with a few of the highlights and struggles in a story of how GOD has used the obedience of two of his children, to be his open arms. In the course of this adventure I have been blessed to see God raise up one man, woman and family after another and confirm my belief that I am not the "Last man standing" but rather Jesus is, and through Him I can do all things.

I am confident of this; He can and will use you to. It may be by reaching out to one child in your neighborhood, getting involved in a mentoring program, encouraging your church to begin working with a struggling school, starting a ministry to single mothers, or volunteering in a national or international children's mission. Whatever form it takes, one thing is sure; GOD will use you, when you obey Him. Believe it.

LAST MAN STANDING

Vision Meets Reality

When we left Northern Virginia in 2006 we went with open hearts and open arms. We were full of dreams and visions about what GOD would do and some romantic notions of what missionary life would be like. We sold our home at the peak of the real estate bubble and were able to arrive in Brazil debt free and with money to invest in starting a brand new ministry among at-risk children. It seemed like a huge gamble to a lot of folks, but we believed that if we sought "first His Kingdom and His righteousness," then GOD would care for our needs. We called it "Open Arms Brazil," a not-for-profit, Christian organization dedicated to the spiritual, emotional, physical and social enrichment of children and youth who live in under-served or forgotten communities - communities where families and children are at higher risk of becoming victims of poverty, crime, violence, addiction, abuse, and social marginalization. The name reflected what we felt GOD had called us to be for these children, namely the "open arms" of Jesus Christ, there to embrace them and help them to embrace the GOD who makes all things new, even broken families, broken homes and broken lives that were on a path to sorrow and death.

GOD had prepared partners for us in the city where we would establish our headquarters, Assis, São Paulo. A Spirit-filled, Independent Presbyterian Church from a neighborhood called Jardim Paulista, along with their church plant in a rough part of town, had come to understand that they, as the body of Christ, are the last man standing and were there to

CHAPTER 8 – OPEN HEARTS, OPEN ARMS

work alongside us, pray with us and struggle with us as this infant mission began to take its first halting steps.

Those early days were a lot like starting a new company. Patricia and I worked around the clock to find a place where we could meet with the children, raise up and train a volunteer team, purchase supplies, develop a teaching plan, and jump through all the bureaucratic hoops necessary to register our organization with the government authorities. For both of us the reality of living in another culture, and all the struggles that entails brought our romantic dreams quickly down to earth. I'll share some of those struggles with you here not as a discouragement, but rather as a heads up. As our Lord promised, "In this world you will have troubles."

The Gideon Treatment

Let me begin by saying that sanctification, godly character development, is a normal part of the Christian life. Sometimes it's happening below the radar of our consciousness. Other times it's like having your wisdom teeth removed without anesthesia. This first struggle was one of those latter times.

You might remember, as recorded in the book of Judges, GOD finally convinced Gideon that he was in fact a "mighty warrior" and now he had 30,000 men at his disposal, ready to attack Midian. He was feeling confident I'm sure.

Right up until GOD said, "No that's too many. Let's cut that back to 20,000." And then again, "Nope, still too many. How about 300? Perfect." What!? That would have been my response I'm afraid. GOD knew that without question this victory would be attributed to Him alone and that Gideon would learn a valuable lesson. The lesson being that, even if you are gifted as a mighty warrior and blessed with resources to go into battle, GOD is still the one who fights for you. Not only is the victory His, but the battle as well. And thus He alone deserves the glory for the outcome.

In my case, GOD took me away from a successful ministry, leaving a place where I had some degree of respect, a place where I could comfortably teach, debate, facilitate meetings, give presentations, counsel and lead public prayer. From that mountaintop He brought to me to a place where my language skills rivaled that of a 5th grader, my vocabulary that of a 2nd grader, and my writing skills, well I don't want to talk about that. I was a mighty warrior with 30,000 men and now look at me!

I questioned, "Oh GOD, why have you muted the gifts you yourself gave me? Why have you taken away all of my fellow soldiers? Why have you sent me into the greatest battle of my life naked?" But there was a quiet voice in my soul that said in reply, "Because I AM the one who fights for you, I AM the one who wins the victory, I AM the one who rightfully deserves the glory, and I know that it is in your eternal best interest to remember these truths my child and I love you."

CHAPTER 8 – OPEN HEARTS, OPEN ARMS

In looking back I see how totally I depended on GOD and how He provided for me, first through my wonderfully talented bride who acted as my Aaron, speaking for me when my Portuguese wasn't up to the task, and then by raising up a new army of friends in Brazil who have grown to become like family to us. All that had been stripped away was restored, to the glory of GOD.

Fish out of water

Some of our struggles were comical. Little things, like opening a bank account or paying a bill, were suddenly an adventure. While Patricia was born and raised in Brazil, her entire adult life was spent in the States. She was as clueless as I was when it came to these simple functions of life and this made for some really funny episodes.

One particular afternoon we took the children to a local government office in our town so that we could have their national identification cards made. The secretary at the front desk handed us the forms. When we asked for a pen she replied, "The forms have to be typed." "OK," we responded, "Do you have a typewriter here? Because we don't have one." "No. We don't," came the answer, "But if you go to the end of the street and turn right, there is a hotdog stand about halfway down on your left and they will fill out the forms for a fee." At this point I couldn't help but laugh out loud because I was sure she was kidding. I wanted to look around for the hidden cameras. Was this "tease the gringo day"? When she didn't share in my amusement, we realized she was serious.

Still somewhat incredulous, we followed her instructions and found the hotdog stand. We stood there with the forms in our hands, completely embarrassed, and wondering what the fry-cook would say when we asked him to fill out our forms. Thankfully we didn't need to ask. When he saw the forms, he wiped off his hands and ducked down only to reappear a moment later grasping an ancient typewriter which he plopped atop the grease truck's window counter. Our 9-year-old son looked, with his head slightly cocked to one side, and said with wonder, "What is THAT?!" He'd never seen a typewriter before!

On another occasion Patricia and I travelled to a neighboring state to purchase a car. We had been told we would find better deals there. We headed out with a borrowed car and $20,000 in cash. Not the brightest idea in a third world country. Approaching a toll plaza far from home, we looked at one another and asked, "Did you bring any Brazilian money?" Now what? We saw a sign that said, "Cards," and assumed it meant debit or credit cards. "Great". The toll attendant stood, looking puzzled at our debit card. "We don't take these. Only our pass cards work here." Between us we had four Brazilian Reais, but the toll was seven. "Will you take dollars?" "No, we can't take dollars." "Can we pay you on our way back?" "No, if you can't pay you'll need to turn around. There is a bank in a town about 15 minutes back down the road though."

CHAPTER 8 – OPEN HEARTS, OPEN ARMS

Well we had no bank account yet, but we went anyway in the hopes that our US debit card might work to withdraw the needed funds (the equivalent of about $1.50 US at the time). The bank had no ATM machine that would accept a US card. We went to the bank manager. Would they exchange dollars? No. Finally Patricia broke down in her frustration and said to the manager, "You mean to tell me, I have $20,000 in my purse and yet I can't get through a toll plaza!?" Sympathizing with our predicament, or maybe just wanting to get rid of us, the manager asked how much we needed, took the change out of his own wallet and sent us on our way. I often refer to the episode as the greatest "devaluation" of the dollar of all time.

In other ways, reality was not so humorous. On September 15 of 2006, I wrote the following in a blog post to our friends and family back home.

"Just one story

Hi Friends,

> *I couldn't sleep tonight. The kids at Braços Abertos (Open Arms) had a good week, but one story has haunted my mind and I can't shake it. Maybe if I share it with you. At least you can pray for this young person. We'll call the child Lucas. I don't want to share the real name or whether this is a boy or girl. It isn't important to the story anyway. All the kids at Bracos Abertos have a story and I am just beginning to learn some of them. This one made*

me cry when it was first relayed to me, and will probably do so again now.

Most of the adults in Lucas' life are drug users and have been his whole life. When Lucas' was only 5 or 6, he and his uncle were home alone when a local drug dealer came to the door to collect a past due debt from the uncle. Lucas' uncle didn't have the money and so was shot repeatedly, in front of the child and died. He spent the day sitting next to the uncle's dead body crying until finally someone came home.

It's been several years now, but he cries to go into school and is terrified of being alone. When Lucas first came to us we met someone who didn't smile and was very timid. By GOD's grace and, I believe, through the love of Christ that is poured out to him from our team of volunteers, he smiles now and laughs and plays. Lucas has even started to go to school.

GOD can heal Lucas' wounds. GOD can make him whole again. I want to see Lucas in heaven clothed in white and walking on streets of gold. It will be so different from where he walks today. Here I go crying again. Please pray for Lucas with me. That's all. Just one story."

CHAPTER 8 – OPEN HEARTS, OPEN ARMS

Naysayers

Like Nehemiah in his day, we had our share of naysayers and opposition along the way as well. As we travelled around the city, looking for space to begin the work, we ran into obstacle after obstacle. Without a space of our own, many well-meaning people said that we should wait to start any activities until we could build or rent an adequate space. We had people who saw no hope for these children and viewed our plans as "wishful thinking" and a "waste of time."

By faith, we chose not to listen to those voices. Despite the spiritual and cultural "giants in the land," we firmly believed in the transforming power of the Gospel and in the calling we had received to start this work. So we stepped out, and in every struggle we were privileged to see GOD act on our behalf to close the mouths of His enemies and bring Himself glory.

In July of 2006 we began to work with about 30 children and 10 volunteers, out of a little one room church building and a two-room house next door. A little later on, the volunteers and children redeemed a vacant, overgrown lot across the street from the church that had become a place for dumping garbage and presented health risks to the surrounding residents. We planted trees, weeded, removed more than ten dumpsters worth of trash, and put up soccer goals, which were donated by the city. In those humble beginnings we began the battle for the souls of the children of one city in Brazil, but it wouldn't end there.

Where there is no way...

As we grew, the community began to take notice. Within a year it was clear just how far into their hearts Open Arms had gotten. In this neighborhood of government built houses, there was a community center; a simple, square, one room structure with a kitchen and bathrooms and surrounded by a significant amount of green space. It had been built for use by the community, but had been abandoned and fallen into disrepair. Everything from the lights, to wiring, to the toilets and plumbing were stolen and the center had become a crash pad for crack users, prostitutes and the homeless.

To us it seemed like the perfect next step for the ministry. The residents were excited about the possibility that this building, which had become a tumor on the face of the neighborhood, might be restored and used to bless their children. A petition was circulated and sent on to the Mayor.

Sure that GOD had given us the building and was redeeming it for Christ, we started making plans. That initial excitement quickly turned to frustration though as local political bickering appeared to squash our dream. The land didn't belong to the city but to the community association. The only entity that could legally cede the use of the building

CHAPTER 8 – OPEN HEARTS, OPEN ARMS

to Open Arms would be the homeowners association. That association had long been disbanded, so in essence we had no legal entity with which to work. It was over. Our last official act in regard to the community center would be to organize a small prayer walk with our volunteers from the local church. After passing through each street in the community, we stopped for a long time in front of that little abandoned building and delivered it into GOD's hands.

GOD makes a way

Less than a year after that prayer, I got a call from a friend in the neighborhood letting me know that some of the residents had gotten so frustrated by what had happened with the petition drive that they had resolved to find a lawyer, and reconstitute the Association Board. "That's great news," I said. "Good for them." At least something positive had come out of that entire struggle.

I didn't give it much more thought but watched as the new Community Association Board raised money and, doing much of the labor themselves, fenced in the property, fixed the broken doors, replaced the window glass, plumbing, wiring, bathroom fixtures, and even purchased a stove and refrigerator. They cut the grass, painted the building and then…made a phone call. The new President of the Community Association called us with an invitation. "Would you please attend our next Board meeting and consider moving your local outreach project to our new community center?" Open Arms would have free use of the space and the athletic fields for as long as we wanted.

In the coming months and years we would work with this small community to plant trees, install curtains, hold outreach events, and finally install a first-class playground. GOD had made a way. He had answered our prayers in a way that none of us expected and which left all the glory for Him and Him alone. That Community Center has been, and continues to be today, the sight of numerous children giving their lives to Jesus and being mentored by loving Christian volunteers who took seriously their position as "last man standing", and committed themselves to being fathers to the fatherless, or Uncles and Aunts, as we are called by the children. But the story doesn't end there either.

A Wider Vision

As GOD continued to bless the ministry and people began to take notice of the transformation occurring in the lives of many of the children, and even the volunteers involved, more of them came to join the cause. Some even came from other cities to see what we were doing and find out how they could do the same. What was our strategy and why did it work? For the first time we began looking closely at how we did things and documenting the lessons learned. Our strategy, inspired by the US Army Green Berets, consists of 8 steps.

CHAPTER 8 – OPEN HEARTS, OPEN ARMS

1. Identifying and studying an at-risk community,
2. Locating a sympathetic body of believers in or adjacent to that community,
3. Winning over the leadership of that local church,
4. Mobilizing its members to join the battle,
5. Helping them identify the redeemable physical and human resources within their community,
6. Training them to carry on the work of the ministry to the at-risk children and the fatherless within their own cultural context,
7. Supplying them with tested curriculum, know-how, and occasionally assisting with financial resources in a limited way, and
8. Ministering alongside them.

As more people came to us we started to see a broader picture come into focus. Maybe GOD was beginning to move in a new way. Perhaps Open Arms could and should become more than one outreach in one neighborhood in Brazil. Perhaps the lessons we had learned the hard way about community-based ministry could help others. Maybe Open Arms Brazil could become an organization that mobilizes, prepares, equips and aids Christian lay leaders in implementing transformational, faith-based, children and youth outreach projects among the world's poor. Not just in one city and not just in Brazil.

Our Board and volunteers in Brazil enthusiastically embraced this vision and before we knew it, there were Open Arms Outreach Projects in five other cities in Brazil spread over four states. We had partnered with five more churches and opened three more outreach points in Assis. The church in North America even began to get involved as we received various short-term missions teams to work with us. The Open Arms field staff grew, increasing our ability to train and equip more volunteers.

In 2010 a new organization, Open Arms Worldwide, was incorporated in the state of Virginia, in order to better fulfill this expanded vision. The Board of that new organization was made up almost entirely of former members of short-term teams that had come to work with us. In July of 2011 the first official leadership preparation course was given by the Open Arms Center for Leadership Training in Assis. Forty lay leaders and five pastors participated in that first class. As of the writing of this book, a video curriculum is being developed to get the training course into the hands of more churches around Brazil.

Our team is praying for opportunities to reach out to other nations as well. Our desire and prayer is to see a new generation that knows the Lord and all that He has done. If it is up to us, we won't see Joshua's mistake repeated.

Our goal is nothing short of EVERY Bible believing church on the planet embracing the call to reach, teach and bless the children in their community and beyond.

In response, GOD has sent, one by one and two by two, talented and passionate people who share His vision for reaching and teaching children. They are too many to name here and the testimonies of transformed lives, and of how GOD has done miraculous things over and over again, would fill up two or three more books.

So it is with great joy that I thank GOD for all that was accomplished over those early years through the ministry of Open Arms. It has grown to include a soccer school, a swim program, a leadership course, and an outreach into the juvenile detention centers of Brazil. Hundreds of children are being pulled away from the influence of drugs, violence, and poverty, being shown a new path and being ministered to on a weekly basis, learning the timeless truths of the Bible and seeing the love of Jesus Christ in action.

Planting Seeds of Hope

As we admire a mighty oak tree in all its grandeur, it can be easy to forget that it started as a tiny seed. The thought that all of that beauty and majesty began as something so small is cause for praise. It is such powerful imagery that it is no wonder the Lord used a similar comparison to describe the Kingdom of Heaven. It is the image that comes to mind when I consider the work the Lord has done, and is doing, in and through Open Arms. In the years that Patricia and I have dedicated to the founding of this ministry in Brazil we have seen a seed planted and begin to germinate. The Christian community in Brazil has begun to awaken to their calling to be the "Last Man Standing" in the fight for a generation. Today we are thrilled to see so many in the body of Christ here in the

U.S. embracing this vision as well. Open Arms Worldwide is hard at work partnering with local Christian churches in North America, mobilizing them to bring the message of hope and a future in Christ to a generation of children who are waiting.

One

Remember that object lesson we started out with, the child crossing a stage full of bear traps? I want you to visualize that again now. Every minute of every day, tens of thousands of children start that journey alone and blindfolded. Will there be someone there to walk with them? You can't help them all but you can help one, and as a church perhaps many more. May GOD give you the courage, strength, wisdom and discernment to be a "Father to the fatherless," the last man standing in the life of a child, and so welcome the presence of Christ into your life.

"And whoever welcomes one such child in my name welcomes me"

- Jesus the Christ (Matthew 18:5)

Discussion Questions

If, after reading this book, you simply put it on the shelf and forget its words, then I have failed. Jesus said the wise man was the one who heard his words and put them into action. You can discard my words, but the commands of Christ you've read in these pages are quite a different thing.

The following questions are meant to act as a starting point for you, your family, and your church family to begin a discussion about how you can respond to GOD's command to reach, teach and stand in the gap for His little ones.

For Church Leadership

1. Have we developed an integrated vision for children, youth and family ministry within our church? If not, why not? If yes, does everyone on staff and in the body understand that vision?

2. Are we satisfied that our ministry is living up to each of the following points? In which ones are we excelling and in which do we need to improve?

- Children of the church need to be recognized as people of faith

- Children need to both contribute and receive as members of GOD's family

- Children must be invited to participate as the church in fellowship, worship, prayer, learning of the Word and service.

- Children need to be changed by the love of Christ and share the Gospel in their context.

- Parents must be equipped within the church to fulfill their role as primary spiritual leaders of their children.

- Our investments in time, talent and treasure should reflect our commitment to these truths.

- Our success can only be measured by the spiritual growth of the children in our sphere of influence

3. What impact is fatherlessness and single motherhood having on our church? Our community?

4. Are, we as a church family, imitating GOD in the way we reach out to the fatherless and the widow? List ways you are doing this and ideas for how you might do better.

5. In our local and international missionary activity, what percentage of our effort is directed at reaching and teaching children for Jesus? Is that adequate, given what we know about how GOD has wired children?

For men of GOD and their families

1. How am I, or are we, seeking GOD's presence and will through service?

2. Dads, how do you rate yourself (be honest) when it comes to the spiritual preparation of your children? Moms, how do you rate dad? Be gentle.

3. Couples, can you think of a fatherless child (either completely or partially so) and/or a single mother that is within your sphere of influence that your family and marriage could potentially impact in positive way? How might you do that?

4. Everyone, are there any ministries within your church or volunteer organizations in your community that focus on at-risk children that you could participate in? If so, how?

5. How can you reorder your life to make room for a mentoring relationship with a young person?

6. How can you reflect a desire to bless the fatherless through your giving habits?

The body of Jesus is all that stands between the children of the world and Satan's schemes. Don't let your journey stall here. Seek out resources and opportunities to be used by GOD. He is calling you into the fight. How you respond will have implications for eternity.

```
You can go online and share
  your experiences with us at
www.lastmanstandingchurch.com
```

About Open Arms Worldwide

Open Arms Worldwide (OAW) is a not-for-profit, Christian organization dedicated to the spiritual, moral, emotional, physical and social enrichment of children and youth who live in under-served or forgotten communities around the world - communities where families and children are at higher risk of becoming victims of poverty, crime, violence, addiction, abuse, and social marginalization.

Open Arms Worldwide (Open Arms) envisions a world where children can grow up understanding that they are beautiful and precious in God's eyes and where they are enabled to discover the hope and future that is possible.

Our Mission

Our Mission is simply to partner with Christian churches to implement and maintain gospel-based programs to reach at-risk children in the church's local community.

Training missionaries, developing discipleship materials, mobilizing more churches, and reaching into more forgotten neighborhoods with the hope of Jesus, all require resources. GOD works through the sacrifices of his saints.

LAST MAN STANDING

Some are called to go, some to stay and build support for those who went, some to give, some to carry the news, and all to pray. What role can you play?

Go to WWW.OPENARMSWORLDWIDE.ORG today to find out how you can make an impact.

About the Author

Michael John Meyers is a man who loves Jesus, loves his family, and has a passion for helping young people find the path that leads to life. In pursuit of that calling, Michael left a successful career in the business world to eventually take on the role of Director of Children's Ministries at Reston Bible Church in Reston, Virginia. In 2005 Michael and his wife Patricia founded Open Arms Brazil. Then, in 2006, they were commissioned by their church and moved to Brazil where they founded Comunidade Braços Abertos Brasil. In 2011 he became the founding President of Open Arms Worldwide (OAW).

Michael is a missionary as well as a speaker and writer. With his mix of private sector business, education, and ministry experience, Michael brings an entrepreneurial approach and outlook to missions, the church and the urgent need for GOD's people to stand in the gap for the next generation. He lives with his wife, Patricia, and their three children, Michael, Raphael & Gabriela in Northern Virginia where he continues to lead the Children's Ministry of their church.

Follow Mike on

http://www.lastmanstandingchurch.com

LAST MAN STANDING

What others are saying

"When you first meet the Meyers, their passion for the children and the communities they work in is so evident it's contagious. You can't help but get excited listening to their story and vision for Open Arms Worldwide... As a nonprofit fundraiser, I am constantly impressed at the direction that OAW is going. Their strategic growth plan and the ways that Mike and Patricia have helped raise and encourage leaders within the community, ensures long-term and sustainable impact within the communities they serve."

- Bindu Balan, Development Manager, Jumpstart Tri-State Region

"Mike Meyers is a visionary in the field of Children's Ministry. He consistently implements creative ideas for effectively communicating the Gospel of Jesus Christ to the next generation. Mike's compassion for the poor and his ability to share this message of hope in engaging ways has impacted lives of countless children for eternity. As a parent who has benefitted from Mike's influence in the lives of my children and as a co-laborer in proclaiming this Good News to today's youth, I would encourage anyone who has a heart for reaching children to leverage Mike's gifting in these areas."

- Jason Goetz, Director of Family Ministry, Reston Bible Church

"The Meyers family has been chosen by God for such a time as this! They are an ordinary family that has joined an extraordinary God in His mission to redeem, renew and restore a broken world. In a day and age when so many Christians are blinded by comfort and security God uses men like Michael to awaken them to God's call on their lives. They are a family who said to the Lord, "send us, we will go no matter what the cost." What would your church or organization look like if they all embraced God's call on their lives like the Meyers family has? We have much to learn from Michael. I thank the Lord for the Meyers family and the example they have been to my family."

-Edward Hunt, Pastor

Made in the USA
Charleston, SC
23 July 2014